Principia Qualia
Volume One: Framework & Valence

Michael Edward Johnson
Qualia Research Institute
johnsonmx@gmail.com

Special thanks[1] to Dr. Randal Koene,
whose mentorship, feedback, and conversations about brains helped make this research happen.[2]

To Dr. Radhika Dirks,
for feedback & editing, physics expertise, encouragement, and wisdom.

To Andres Gomez Emilsson,
who saw the full problem, rolled up his sleeves, and worked on it.

And to my family & Lili Mao.

Thanks also to Giego Caleiro, Scott Jackisch, Romeo Stevens, Anthony Rudd, Stephen Frey, Adam Safron, Joshua Vogelstein, Duncan Wilson, Mark Lippman, Emily Crotteau, Eli Tyre, Andrew Lapinski-Barker, Allan Herman-Pool, Anatoly Karlin, Alex Alekseyenko, Leopold Haller, and Brian Westerman for offering helpful feedback on drafts along the way.

---

[1] Except as noted the views herein are my own, and the above acknowledgements of contribution do not imply endorsements of my positions.
[2] The background arguments about brains and IIT were significantly aided by an extensive series of collaborative meetings with Dr. Koene, and will also form the basis for another joint publication.

Abstract:

Philosophers have been wondering the nature of consciousness (what it feels like to have subjective experience) and qualia (individual components of subjective experience) for as long as Philosophy has existed. Advancements in physics and neuroscience have informed and constrained this mystery, but have not solved it. What would a *systematic* solution to the mystery of consciousness look like?

Part I begins by grounding this topic by considering a concrete question: what makes some conscious experiences more pleasant than others? We first review what's known about the neuroscience of pain & pleasure, find the current state of knowledge narrow, inconsistent, and often circular, and conclude we must look elsewhere for a systematic framework (Sections I & II). We then review the Integrated Information Theory (IIT) of consciousness and several variants of IIT, and find each of them promising, yet also underdeveloped and flawed (Sections III-V).

We then take a step back and distill what kind of problem consciousness *is*. Importantly, we offer eight sub-problems whose solutions would, in aggregate, constitute a *complete theory of consciousness* (Section VI).

Armed with this framework, in Part II we return to the subject of pain & pleasure (valence) and offer some assumptions, distinctions, and heuristics to clarify and constrain the problem (Sections VII-IX). Of <u>particular interest, we then offer a specific hypothesis on what valence *is*</u> (Section X) and several novel empirical predictions which follow from this (Section XI). Part III finishes with discussion of how this general approach may inform open problems in neuroscience, and the prospects for building a new science of qualia (Sections XII & XIII). Lastly, we identify further research threads within this framework (Appendices A-F).

Introduction:
Some experiences feel better than others, and this informs and undergirds everything about the human condition. But why-- what *makes* some experiences better than others? This question has been a recurring puzzle, posed in various forms by e.g., Epicurus, Shakespeare, Jeremy Bentham, and affective neuroscience. But despite literal millennia of research, we know an embarrassingly small amount about the mechanisms and metaphysics behind it, and there's little agreement on even what a proper answer should *look* like. We can call this the problem of *valence*.

I believe there's a *rigorous, crisp,* and relatively *simple* solution to this puzzle, but there's a lot of theoretical scaffolding that needs to be put in place first. Part 1 reviews what is known and the leading quantitative hypotheses about valence, qualia and consciousness, with a focus on affective neuroscience and IIT. I end this section by summarizing and synthesizing a framework for understanding consciousness research in terms of modular, granular sub-problems. Part 2 directly addresses valence as a sub-problem in consciousness research, offers a hypothesis as to what valence *is*, and suggests specific empirical tests of the hypothesis. In Part 3 we discuss further predictions, implications, practical applications and current relevance.

Finally, in the appendices we describe how to grow this approach into a *formal science of qualia*.

Readers with a strong grasp of the literature on valence and on IIT, or those wanting to quickly get to the heart of the argument, should feel free to jump to Section VI.

Contents
Part I - Review
I. Why some things feel better than others: the view from neuroscience
II. Clarifying the Problem of Valence
III. The *Integrated Information Theory* of consciousness (IIT)
IV. Critiques of IIT
V. Alternative versions of IIT: Perceptronium and FIIH
VI. Summary and synthesis: eight problems for a new science of consciousness

Part II - Valence
VII. Three principles for a mathematical derivation of valence
VIII. Distinctions in qualia: charting the explanation space for valence
IX. Summary of heuristics for reverse-engineering the pattern for valence
X. A simple hypothesis about valence
XI. Testing this hypothesis today

Part III - Discussion
XII. Taking Stock
XIII. Closing thoughts
Appendices A-F

Part I - Review

I. Why some things feel better than others: the view from neuroscience

Affective neuroscience has been very effective at illuminating the dynamics and correlations of how valence works in the human brain, on a *practical* level, and what valence is *not*, on a *metaphysical* level. This is *useful* yet not *philosophically rigorous*, and this trend is likely to continue.

Valence research tends to segregate into two buckets: *function* and *anatomy*. The former attempts to provide a description of how valence interacts with thought and behavior, whereas the latter attempts to map it to the anatomy of the human brain. The following are key highlights from each 'bucket':

Valence as a functional component of thought & behavior:

One of the most common views of valence is that it's the way the brain encodes *value*:
> Emotional feelings (*affects*) are intrinsic values that inform animals how they are faring in the quest to survive. The various positive affects indicate that animals are returning to "comfort zones" that support survival, and negative affects reflect "discomfort zones" that indicate that animals are in situations that may impair survival. They are ancestral tools for living - evolutionary memories of such importance that they were coded into the genome in rough form (as primary brain processes), which are refined by basic learning mechanisms (secondary processes) as well as by higher-order cognitions/thoughts (tertiary processes). (Panksepp 2010).

Similarly, valence seems to be a mechanism the brain uses to determine or label *salience*, or phenomena worth paying attention to (J. C. Cooper and Knutson 2008), and to drive reinforcement learning (Bischoff-Grethe et al. 2009).

A common thread in these theories is that valence is entangled with, and perhaps caused by, an *appraisal* of a situation. Frijda describes this idea as *the law of situated meaning*: "Input some event with its particular meaning; out comes an emotion of a particular kind" (Frijda 1988). Similarly, Clore et al. phrase this in terms of "The Information Principle", where "[e]motional feelings provide conscious information from unconscious appraisals of situations." (Clore, Gasper, and Garvin 2001) Within this framework, positive valence is generally modeled as the result of an outcome being *better than expected* (Schultz 2015), or a surprising decrease in 'reward prediction errors' (RPEs) (Joffily and Coricelli 2013).

Computational affective neuroscience is a relatively new subdiscipline which attempts to formalize this appraisal framework into a unified model of cognitive-emotional-behavioral dynamics. A good example is "Mood as Representation of Momentum" (Eldar et al. 2016), where moods (and valence states) are understood as *pre-packaged behavioral and epistemic biases* which can be applied to different strategies depending on what kind of 'reward prediction errors' are occurring. E.g., if things are going *surprisingly well*, the brain tries to take advantage of this momentum by shifting into a happier state that is more suited to exploration & exploitation. On the other hand, if things are going *surprisingly poorly*, the brain shifts into a "hunker-down" mode which conserves resources and options.

However- while these functional descriptions are intuitive, elegant, and appear to explain quite a lot about valence, frustratingly, they fall apart as *metaphysically-satisfying answers* when we look closely at edge-cases and the *anatomy* of pain and pleasure.

Valence as a product of neurochemistry & neuroanatomy:

The available neuroanatomical evidence suggests that the above functional themes merely highlight *correlations* rather than *metaphysical truths*, and for every *functional* story about the role of valence, there exist counter-examples. E.g.:

<u>Valence is not the same as value or salience:</u>
(Berridge and Kringelbach 2013) find that "representation [of value] and causation [of pleasure] may actually reflect somewhat separable neuropsychological functions". Relatedly, (Jensen et al. 2007) note that *salience* is also handled by different, non-perfectly-overlapping systems in the brain.

<u>Valence should not be thought of in terms of preferences, or reinforcement learning:</u>
Even more interestingly, (Berridge, Robinson, and Aldridge 2009) find that what we call 'reward' has three distinct elements in the brain: *'wanting', 'liking', and 'learning'*, and the neural systems supporting each are each relatively distinct from each other. 'Wanting', a.k.a. seeking, seems strongly (though not wholly) dependent upon the mesolimbic dopamine system, whereas 'liking', or the actual subjective experience of pleasure, seems to depend upon the opioid, endocannabinoid, and GABA-benzodiazepine neurotransmitter systems, but only within the context of a handful of so-called "hedonic hotspots" (elsewhere, their presence seems to only increase 'wanting'). With the right interventions disabling each system, it looks like brains can exhibit any permutation of these three: 'wanting and learning without liking', 'wanting and liking without learning', and so on. Likewise with pain, we can roughly separate the sensory/discriminative component from the affective/motivational component, each of which can be modulated independently (Shriver 2016).

These distinctions between components are empirically significant but not necessarily theoretically crisp: (Berridge and Kringelbach 2013) suggest that the dopamine-mediated, novelty-activated seeking state of mind involves at least some small amount of intrinsic pleasure.

A strong theme in the affective neuroscience literature is that pleasure seems highly linked to certain specialized brain regions / types of circuits:
> We note the rewarding properties for all pleasures are likely to be generated by hedonic brain circuits that are distinct from the mediation of other features of the same events (e.g., sensory, cognitive). Thus pleasure is never merely a sensation or a thought, but is instead an additional hedonic gloss generated by the brain via dedicated systems. … Analogous to scattered islands that form a single archipelago, hedonic hotspots are anatomically distributed but interact to form a functional integrated circuit. The circuit obeys control rules that are largely hierarchical and organized into brain levels. Top levels function together as a cooperative heterarchy, so that, for example, multiple unanimous 'votes' in favor from simultaneously-participating hotspots in the nucleus accumbens and ventral pallidum are required for opioid stimulation in either forebrain site to enhance 'liking' above normal. (Kringelbach and Berridge 2009)

Some of these 'hedonic hotspots' are also implicated in pain, and activity in normally-hedonic regions have been shown to produce an aversive effect under certain psychological conditions, e.g., when threatened or satiated (Berridge and Kringelbach 2013). Furthermore, damage to certain regions of the brain (e.g., the ventral pallidum) in rats changes their reaction toward normally-pleasurable things to active 'disliking' (Cromwell and Berridge 1993; K. S. Smith et al. 2009). Moreover, certain painkillers such as acetaminophen blunt both pain *and* pleasure (Durso, Luttrell, and Way 2015). By implication, the circuits or activity patterns that cause pain and pleasure may have similarities not shared with 'hedonically neutral' circuits. However, pain does seem to be a slightly more 'distributed' phenomenon than pleasure, with fewer regions that consistently contribute.

Importantly, the key takeaway from the neuro-anatomical research into valence is this: at this time *we don't have a clue as to what properties are necessary or sufficient to make a given brain region a so-called "pleasure center" or "pain center"*. Instead, we just know that some regions of the brain appear to contribute much more to valence than others.

Finally, the core circuitry implicated in emotions in general, and valence in particular, is highly evolutionarily conserved, and all existing brains seem to generate valence in similar ways: "Cross-species affective neuroscience studies confirm that primary-process emotional feelings are organized within primitive subcortical regions of the brain that are anatomically, neurochemically, and functionally homologous in all mammals that have been studied." (Panksepp 2010) Others have indicated the opioid-mediated 'liking' reaction may be conserved across an incredibly broad range of brains, from the very complex (humans & other mammals) to the very simple (*c. elegans*, with 302 neurons), and all known data points in between- e.g., vertebrates, molluscs, crustaceans, and insects (D'iakonova 2001). On the other hand, the role of dopamine may be substantially different, and even behaviorally inverted (associated with negative valence and aversion) in certain invertebrates like insects (Van Swinderen and Andretic 2011) and octopi.

A taxonomy of valence?

How many types of pain and pleasure are there? While neuroscience doesn't offer a crisp taxonomy, there are some apparent distinctions we can draw from physiological & phenomenological data:
- There appear to be at least three general types of physical pain, each associated with a certain profile of ion channel activation: thermal (heat, cold, capsaicin), chemical (lactic acid buildup), and mechanical (punctures, abrasions, etc) (Osteen et al. 2016).
- More speculatively, based on a dimensional analysis of psychoactive substances, there appear to be at least three general types of pleasure: 'fast' (cocaine, amphetamines), 'slow' (morphine), and 'spiritual' (LSD, Mescaline, DMT) (Gomez Emilsson 2015b).
- Mutations in the gene SCN9A can remove the ability to feel any pain mediated by physical nociception (Marković, Janković, and Veselinović 2015; Drenth and Waxman 2007)- however, it appears that this doesn't impact the ability to feel emotional pain (Heckert 2012).

However, these distinctions between different types of pain & pleasure appear substantially *artificial*:
- Hedonic pleasure, social pleasure, eudaimonic well-being, etc all seem to be manifestations of the same underlying process. (Kringelbach and Berridge 2009) note: "The available evidence suggests that brain mechanisms involved in fundamental pleasures (food and sexual pleasures) overlap with those for higher-order pleasures (for example, monetary, artistic, musical, altruistic, and transcendent pleasures)." This seems to express a rough neuroscientific consensus (Kashdan, Robert, and King 2008), albeit with some caveats.
- Likewise in support of lumping emotional & physical valence together, common painkillers such as acetaminophen help with both physical and social pain (Dewall et al. 2010).

A deeper exploration of the taxonomy of valence is hindered by the fact that the physiologies of pain and pleasure are frustrating inverses of each other.
- The core hurdle to understanding pleasure (in contrast to pain) is that there's no pleasure-specific circuitry analogous to nociceptors, sensors on the *periphery* of the nervous system which reliably cause pleasure, and whose physiology we can isolate and reverse-engineer.
- The core hurdle to understanding pain (in contrast to pleasure) is that there's only weak and conflicting evidence for pain-specific circuitry analogous to hedonic hotspots, regions deep in the *interior* of the nervous system which seem to centrally coordinate all pain, and whose physiological mechanics & dynamics we can isolate and reverse-engineer.

I.e., pain is easy to cause, but hard to localize in the brain; pleasure has a more definite footprint in the brain, but is much harder to generate on demand.

Philosophical confusion in valence research:

In spite of the progress affective neuroscience continues to make, our current understanding of valence and consciousness is extremely limited, and I offer that the core hurdle for affective neuroscience is philosophical confusion, not mere lack of data. I.e., perhaps our entire approach deserves to be questioned. Several critiques stand out:

Neuroimaging is a poor tool for gathering data:

Much of what we know about valence in the brain has been informed by functional imaging techniques such as fMRI and PET. But neuroscientist Martha Farah notes that these techniques depend upon a very large set of assumptions, and that there's a widespread worry in neuroscience "that [functional brain] images are more researcher inventions than researcher observations." (Farah 2014) Farah notes the following flaws:

- *Neuroimaging is built around indirect and imperfect proxies.* Blood flow (which fMRI tracks) and metabolic rates (which PET tracks) are correlated with neural activity, but exactly *how* and *to what extent* it's correlated is unclear, and skeptics abound. Psychologist William Uttal suggests that "fMRI is as distant as the galvanic skin response or pulse rate from cognitive processes." (Uttal 2011)
- *The elegant-looking graphics neuroimaging produces are not direct pictures of anything: rather, they involve extensive statistical guesswork and 'cleaning actions' by many layers of algorithms.* This hidden inferential distance can lead to unwarranted confidence, especially when most models can't control for differences in brain anatomy.
- *Neuroimaging tools bias us toward the wrong sorts of explanations.* As Uttal puts it, neuroimaging encourages hypotheses "at the wrong (macroscopic) level of analysis rather than the (correct) microscopic level. … we are doing what we can do when we cannot do what we should do." (Uttal 2011)

Neuroscience's methods for analyzing data aren't as good as people think:

There's a popular belief that if only the above data-gathering problems could be solved, neuroscience would be on firm footing. (Jonas and Kording 2016) attempted to test whether the field is merely data-limited (yet has good methods) in a novel way: by taking a microprocessor (where the ground truth is well-known, and unlimited amounts of arbitrary data can be gathered) and attempting to reverse-engineer it via standard neuroscientific techniques such as lesion studies, whole-processor recordings, pairwise & granger causality, and dimensionality reduction. This should be an *easier* task than reverse-engineering brain function, yet when they performed this analysis, they found that "the approaches reveal interesting structure in the data but do not meaningfully describe the hierarchy of information processing in the processor. This suggests that current approaches in neuroscience may fall short of producing meaningful models of the brain." The authors conclude that we don't understand the brain as well as we think we do, and we'll need better theories and methods to get there, not just more data.

Subjective experience is hard to study objectively:

Unfortunately, even if we improved our methods for understanding the brain's *computational hierarchy*, it will be difficult to translate this into improved knowledge of *subjective* mental states & properties of experience (such as valence).

In studying consciousness we've had to rely on either crude behavioral proxies, or subjective reports of what we're experiencing. These 'subjective reports of qualia' are very low-bandwidth, are of unknown reliability and likely vary in complex, hidden ways across subjects, and as (Tsuchiya et al. 2015) notes, the methodological challenge of gathering them "has biased much of the neural correlates of consciousness (NCC) research away from consciousness and towards neural correlates of perceptual reports". I.e., if we ask someone to press a button when they have a certain sensation, then measure their brain activity, we'll often measure the brain activity associated with pressing buttons, rather than the activity associated with the sensation we're interested in. We can and do attempt to control for this with the addition of 'no-report' paradigms, but largely they're based on the sorts of neuroimaging paradigms critiqued above.

Affective neuroscience has confused goals:

Lisa Barrett (L. F. Barrett 2006) goes further and suggests that studying emotions is a *particularly* hard task for neuroscience, since most emotions are not "natural kinds" i.e.. things whose objective existence makes it possible to discover durable facts about. Instead, Barrett notes, "the natural-kind view of emotion may be the result of an error of arbitrary aggregation. That is, our perceptual processes lead us to aggregate emotional processing into categories that do not necessarily reveal the causal structure of the emotional processing." As such, many of the terms we use to speak about emotions have only an ad-hoc, fuzzy pseudo-existence, and this significantly undermines the ability of affective neuroscience to standardize on definitions, methods, and goals.

In summary, affective neuroscience suffers from (1) a lack of tools that gather unbiased and functionally-relevant data about the brain, (2) a lack of formal methods which can reconstruct *what* the brain's doing and *how* it's doing it, (3) epistemological problems interfacing with the subjective nature of consciousness, and (4) an ill-defined *goal,* as it's unclear just what it's attempting to reverse-engineer in the first place.

Fig 1 summarizes some core implications of current neuroscience and philosophical research. In short: valence in the human brain is a complex phenomenon which defies simple description, and affective neuroscience- though it's been hugely useful at illuminating the *shape* of this complexity- is unlikely to generate any sudden or substantial breakthroughs on the topic. But I don't think *valence itself* is necessarily a complex phenomenon, and just because the methodology of affective neuroscience isn't generating crisp insights doesn't mean there are no crisp insights to be had. Section II suggests an alternate way to frame the problem.

Valence is often:	... but this isn't a perfect description, since:
How the brain represents value	It's only a correlation, and 'value' is a fuzzy abstraction
How the brain represents salience	It's only a correlation, and 'salience' is a fuzzy abstraction
A result of getting what we want	'Liking' and 'wanting' are handled by different brain systems
Involved with reinforcement learning	'Liking' and 'learning' are handled by different brain systems
Proximately caused by opioids	Injection of opioids into key regions doesn't always cause pleasure
Proximately caused by certain brain regions	Activity in these regions doesn't always cause pleasure

Figure 1, core takeaways of affective neuroscience on valence

II. Clarifying the Problem of Valence

The above section noted that affective neuroscience knows a lot about valence, but its knowledge is very messy and disorganized. If valence is *intrinsically* a messy, fuzzy property of conscious states, perhaps this really is the best we can do here.

However, I don't think we live in a universe where valence is a fuzzy, fragile, high-level construction. Instead, I think it's a *crisp* thing we can quantify, and the patterns in it only look incredibly messy because we're looking at it from the wrong level of abstraction.

Brains vs conscious systems:

There are fundamentally two *kinds* of knowledge about valence: things that are true specifically in *brains like ours,* and general principles common to *all conscious entities*. Almost all of what we know about pain and pleasure is of the first type-- essentially, affective neuroscience has been synonymous with making maps of the mammalian brain's evolved, adaptive affective modules and contingent architectural quirks ("spandrels").

This paper attempts to chart a viable course for this *second* type of research: it's an attempt toward a *general* theory of valence, a.k.a. universal, substrate-independent principles that apply equally to and are precisely true in *all* conscious entities, be they humans, non-human animals, aliens, or conscious artificial intelligence (AI).

In order to generalize valence research in this way, we need to understand valence research as a subset of qualia research, and qualia research as a problem in information theory and/or physics, rather than neuroscience. Such a generalized approach avoids focusing on contingent facts and instead seeks general *principles* for how the causal organization of a physical system generates or corresponds to its phenomenology, or how it feels to subjectively *be* that system. David Chalmers has hypothesized about this in terms of "psychophysical laws" (Chalmers 1995), or translational principles which we could use to *derive* a system's qualia, much like we can derive the electromagnetic field generated by some electronic gadget purely from knowledge of the gadget's internal composition and circuitry.

In other words, if we want a *crisp, rigorous* definition of valence, we'll have to first address more general questions of consciousness and qualia head-on. There is no road to understanding valence that doesn't also go through understanding consciousness.

-->Definitions:
'Consciousness' is a term often used as a synonym for self-awareness, or for social coordination of internal states, but I'm using it in a limited, technical sense: a system has consciousness if *it feels like something to be that system*. I.e., something is conscious if and only if it has subjective experience.
'Qualia' refers to the elements of consciousness, e.g., redness.

Top-down vs <u>bottom-up</u> theories of consciousness:

There are two basic classes of consciousness theories: top-down (aka 'higher-order' or 'cognitive' theories) and bottom-up. Top-down theories are constructed around the phenomenology of consciousness (i.e., how consciousness *feels*) as well as the high-level dynamics of how the brain implements what we experience.

Top-down approaches have their strengths: they tend to be intuitively legible, manipulable, and are useful as big-picture maps, intuition pumps, and rough-and-ready schemas. Global Workspace (Baars 1988), (Baars 2005) is probably the best known attempt at a top-down, high-level description of how the brain's computational dynamics could correspond with various features of consciousness, where consciousness is modeled as a sort of 'active spotlight' which shines on whatever tasks our brains are prioritizing at the moment. These top-down theories use relatively *high-level* psychological concepts/experiences as their basic ontology or primitives.

However, if we're looking for a solid foundation for any sort of crisp quantification of qualia, top-down theories will almost certainly *not* get us there, since we have no reason to expect that our high-level internal phenomenology has any crisp, intuitive correspondence with the underlying physics and organizational principles which give rise to it. This suggests that theories of consciousness or valence which take high-level psychological concepts as primitives will be "leaky abstractions"[3] (that is to say, we should have very low expectation of a perfect isomorphism between such high-level/top-down theories and reality).[4] Nor are such top-down accounts always *testable*: they're closer to qualitative stories which highlight various aspects of consciousness than quantitative models, although it can be easy to mistake their intuitive legibility for something more formal.[5]

---

[3] A core problem facing theories of mind is that we haven't found any properties that are *well-defined at all levels of abstraction* (e.g., at the levels of neurons, cognition *and* phenomenology). Finding something that is would greatly help us to build bridges between these realms of theory. Valence is a promising candidate here.
[4] Our intuitions about consciousness seem optimized for *adaptedness*, not *truth*, and may in fact be systematically biased away from accuracy in certain ways (see, e.g., work by Dennett).
[5] E.g., consider Douglas Hofstadter's notion that "the mind is a strange loop." It feels compelling, but doesn't seem to predict anything new.

Instead, if we're after a theory of valence/qualia/phenomenology as rigorous as a physical theory, it seems necessary to take the same bottom-up style of approach as physics does when trying to explain something like charge, spin, or electromagnetism. We'll need to start with a handful of primitives that seem unavoidable, indivisible, and unambiguous, and try to find some mathematical approach from which all the high-level phenomenology could naturally emerge. A good rule-of-thumb to distinguish between *bottom-up/rigorous* vs *high-level/leaky* theories of consciousness is that the former kind should apply clearly and equally to any arbitrary cubic foot of space-time, and offer testable predictions at multiple levels of abstraction, whereas the latter may only apply to human sorts of minds in non-esoteric or edge-case scenarios.

For now, the set of bottom-up, fully-mathematical models of consciousness has one subset: Giulio Tononi's Integrated Information Theory (IIT) and IIT-inspired approaches.

So far this paper has been arguing that if we want a *truly crisp* understanding of valence, we need a theory *like* IIT. So what *is* IIT?

III. The *Integrated Information Theory* of consciousness

The neuroscientist Giulio Tononi has argued that, to figure out consciousness, we first must start with the phenomenology of experience- what it *feels* like- and then figure out *principles* for how physical systems would have to be arranged in order to produce the invariants in phenomenology. In the late 2000s Tononi set out to build a formal theory around this approach, and the result is the Integrated Information Theory (IIT) of consciousness.

The central assumption of IIT is that *systems are conscious to the exact degree their dynamics encode integrated information.* "Integrated information," in this context, is information[6] which can't be localized in the system's individual parts over time (IIT calls this *amount* of integrated information the system's "Φ"). Essentially, IIT is a **mathematical transformation function**: give it a circuit diagram of a system (e.g., a brain's connectome), and based on how causally entangled each part is with each other part, IIT will give you something intended to be a mathematical representation of that system's qualia.

A full treatment of IIT is beyond the scope of this work, but see primary works (Balduzzi and Tononi 2008; Tononi 2012; Oizumi, Albantakis, and Tononi 2014; Tononi and Koch 2015), variants (A. B. Barrett 2014; Tegmark 2015), and criticisms (Aaronson 2014a; M. A. Cerullo 2015). The following will be a relatively brief, high-level overview.

<u>IIT's foundation:</u>
Tononi starts with five axiomatic properties that all conscious experiences seem to have. IIT then takes these *axioms* ("essential properties shared by all experiences") and translates them into *postulates*, or physical requirements for conscious physical systems- i.e., "how does the physical world have to be arranged to account for these properties?" (Tononi and Albantakis 2014).

---

[6] Tononi calls this quantity 'intrinsic information', to distinguish this from Shannon's definition of information (which deals with messages, transmission channels, and resolution of uncertainty).

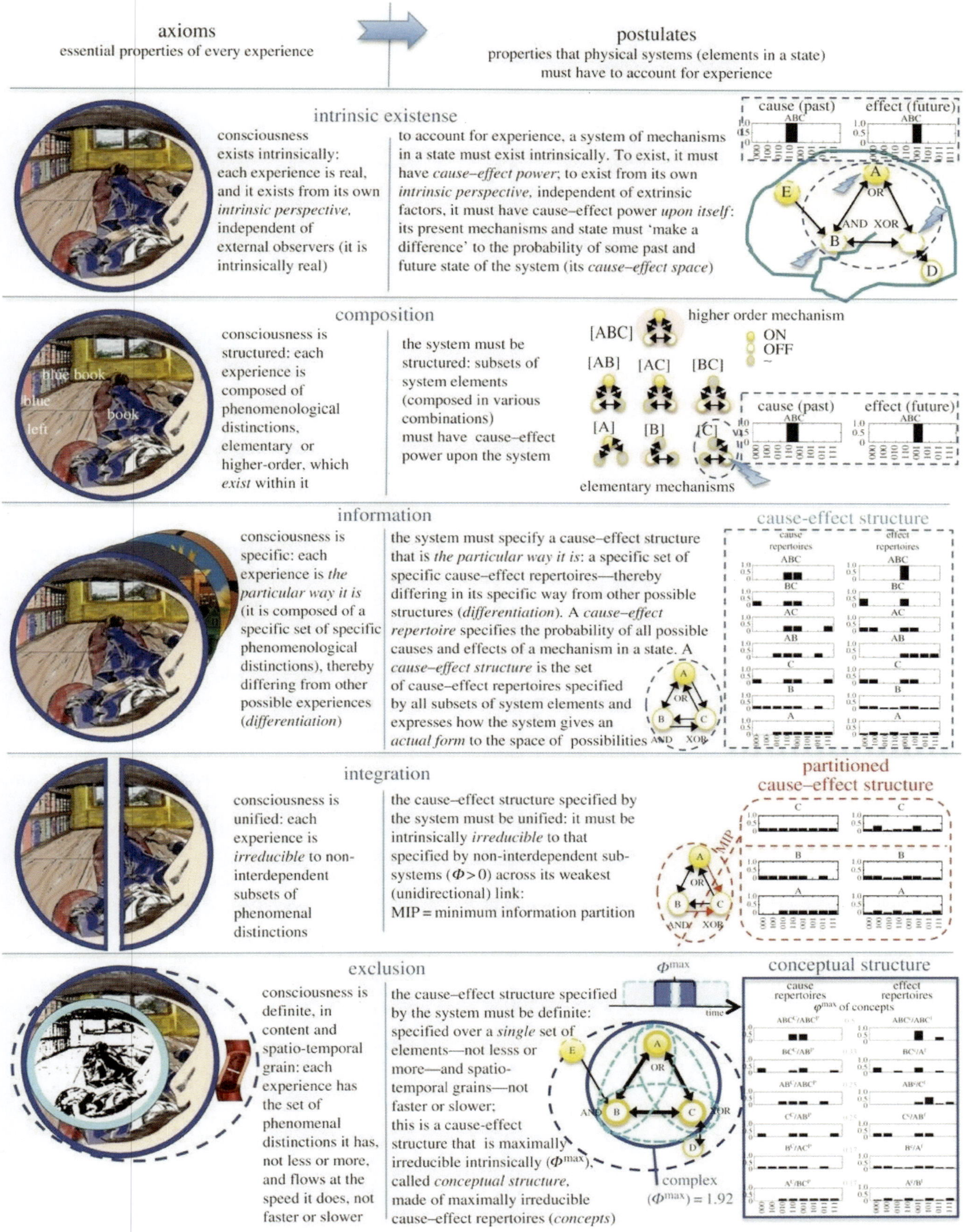

axioms		postulates	
essential properties of every experience		*properties that physical systems (elements in a state) must have to account for experience*	

intrinsic existence

consciousness exists intrinsically: each experience is real, and it exists from its own *intrinsic perspective*, independent of external observers (it is intrinsically real)

to account for experience, a system of mechanisms in a state must exist intrinsically. To exist, it must have *cause–effect power*; to exist from its own *intrinsic perspective*, independent of extrinsic factors, it must have cause–effect power *upon itself*: its present mechanisms and state must 'make a difference' to the probability of some past and future state of the system (its *cause–effect space*)

composition

consciousness is structured: each experience is composed of phenomenological distinctions, elementary or higher-order, which *exist* within it

the system must be structured: subsets of system elements (composed in various combinations) must have cause–effect power upon the system

information

consciousness is specific: each experience is *the particular way it is* (it is composed of a specific set of specific phenomenological distinctions), thereby differing from other possible experiences (*differentiation*)

the system must specify a cause–effect structure that is *the particular way it is*: a specific set of specific cause–effect repertoires—thereby differing in its specific way from other possible structures (*differentiation*). A *cause–effect repertoire* specifies the probability of all possible causes and effects of a mechanism in a state. A *cause–effect structure* is the set of cause–effect repertoires specified by all subsets of system elements and expresses how the system gives an *actual form* to the space of possibilities

integration

consciousness is unified: each experience is *irreducible* to non-interdependent subsets of phenomenal distinctions

the cause–effect structure specified by the system must be unified: it must be intrinsically *irreducible* to that specified by non-interdependent sub-systems ($\Phi > 0$) across its weakest (unidirectional) link: MIP = minimum information partition

exclusion

consciousness is definite, in content and spatio-temporal grain: each experience has the set of phenomenal distinctions it has, not less or more, and flows at the speed it does, not faster or slower

the cause–effect structure specified by the system must be definite: specified over a *single* set of elements—not lesss or more—and spatio-temporal grains—not faster or slower; this is a cause-effect structure that is maximally irreducible intrinsically (Φ^{max}), called *conceptual structure*, made of maximally irreducible cause–effect repertoires (*concepts*)

Figure 2: IIT's axioms and their corresponding postulates. Figure from (Tononi and Koch 2015).

Lastly, based on these postulates, Tononi and Koch have formalized a mathematical *algorithm* for deriving a system's phenomenology from its causal structure.

IIT's goal:
IIT avoids the "Hard Problem" of consciousness (*why* consciousness exists[7]), but aims to address what Scott Aaronson calls the "Pretty-Hard Problem" of consciousness. In a recent internet discussion, Aaronson, Chalmers, and Griffith defined the following hierarchy of 'pretty-hard problems':
- PHP1: "Construct a theory that matches our intuitions about which systems are conscious."
- PHP2: "Construct a theory that tells us which systems are conscious."
- PHP3.5: "Construct a theory that tells us the magnitude of a system's consciousness."
- PHP4: "Construct a theory that tells us which systems have which states of consciousness."

Most people (including Tononi) talk about IIT only in terms of how it does on PHP3.5, but what the most recent version of IIT *actually* does is attempt PHP4 - in formal terms, IIT's goal is to construct a mathematical object isomorphic to a system's qualia.

This is a clear and simple goal, and a great antidote to much of the murky confusion surrounding consciousness research.[8]

IIT's mechanics and output:
IIT defines 'integrated information' as the degree to which activity in each part of a system constrains the activity elsewhere in the system. In highly integrated systems (such as the brain), activity in one part of the brain will affect activity in many other parts.

IIT attempts to formally *measure* this with the following:
(1) First, IIT *deconstructs* a complex causal system into the power set of its internal causal relations. A list of all possible past and future states is calculated for each of these subsets.
(2) Second, each of these subsets is measured to find the one whose current state most highly constrains its past and future states (and thus has the most integrated information). IIT calls this the "Minimum Information Partition" (MIP), and argues that *this specific subset* is where to draw the line for what directly contributes toward the system's consciousness.
(3) Finally, IIT takes this MIP and reorganizes it based on causal clustering into a *geometric figure* within a specially constructed vector space, which Tononi calls "cause-effect space". This geometric figure is intended to represent the phenomenology of how it feels to be the system. Importantly, the *height* of this figure, which Tononi has labeled Φ, corresponds to its amount of integrated information, and thus is *the degree to which the system is conscious*.

IIT can apply at many scales- nanoscale, intracellular, intercellular, groups of neurons, or even larger- but it *chooses which scale matters for subjective experience based on "the spatial grain (& temporal grain and state) associated with a maximum of Φ"* (Tononi and Albantakis 2014). This is important, and ambiguous (see Section IV and Appendix C).

Evidence for IIT:

---

[7] The standard of explanation implied by the Hard Problem may be too much to ask of any physical theory, especially right out of the gate. E.g., we didn't, and still don't, count General Relativity as worthless simply because it failed to explain *why* gravity exists.
[8] If this is the right goal, then we can get on with trying to achieve it. If it's the wrong goal, the onus is now on critics to explain *why*.

Proving or disproving a theory of consciousness seems difficult, without direct access to others' subjective experience. However, Tononi argues that IIT has "predictive, explanatory, and inferential power" and has offered the following evidence in support of IIT:

Intuitively, IIT's five starting postulates seem necessary, and integrated information seems reasonable as a key sort of complexity consciousness could depend upon. It's fairly easy to see that humans seem to have a lot of this sort of complexity, whereas most things we view as not-conscious don't.

Empirically, IIT seems nicely predictive of consciousness under various altered states: e.g., integration (as measured by a TMS and EEG-based perturbation->measurement process) is relatively high during wakefulness, decreases during slow-wave sleep, and rises during REM sleep (Massimini et al. 2005), (Ferrarelli et al. 2010) and is lower in vegetative coma patients than those that later wake up (Casali et al. 2013). Similarly, IIT seems to present a principled connectivity-based rationale for why some brain regions (e.g., the thalamus) seem to generate consciousness, whereas others (e.g., the cerebellum) don't.

Furthermore, under simulations of problem-solving agents, Φ seems to increases as evolved complexity and problem-solving capacity increases: (Albantakis et al. 2014)" found that "The more difficult the task, the higher integrated information in the fittest animats" and concluded "Integrating information is potentially valuable in environments with complex causal structures." From here, it's not a terrible stretch to say that the integrated information and the potential for adaptive (intelligent) behavior of a system are usually highly coupled. This matches the common intuition that intelligence and consciousness go together.

<u>Implications & odds and ends:</u>
The beauty of IIT as a formalized theory is that we don't have to take Tononi's word for what it means: we can apply his equations to arbitrary systems and see what happens. It turns out IIT implies some surprising things:

First, I/O complexity and internal complexity are *usually* good proxies for the Φ of a system, but not always. A complex feed-forward neural network can be highly complex, but because it has no integration between its layers, it has zero Φ. Importantly, *functionally-identical systems* (in terms of I/O) *can produce different qualia* under IIT, depending on their internal structure, and *functionally different* systems may produce the same qualia (Balduzzi and Tononi 2009). However, most systems have at least a little bit of consciousness. E.g., even a photodiode would have a tiny Φ, if structured correctly. Tononi is emphatic that "it's the cause-effect *power* that matters, not what neurons actually do" (Tononi 2016), i.e. how much past states constrain future states, and so he thinks even a system that was totally inactive (e.g., no neurons firing during some time intervals) could have consciousness.

Interestingly, Tononi thinks there might be multiple 'Minimum Information Partitions' within a single human brain: "In addition to 'us', there are going to be some other consciousness within our brain. How big- I mean, how high Φ, and what they are like, I have no idea, but I suspect it's not going to be zero. And I think in some psychiatric conditions like dissociative disorders, it's quite intriguing that some of these may actually not be that small." (Tononi and Albantakis 2014) Though Tononi doesn't explicitly say this, it's possible that which part of the brain contributes to consciousness might move around[9], as the relative levels of integration (Φ) shift- and perhaps certain emotions correspond to 'what it feels like to be a certain brain region'. However, some parts of the brain are simply wired for (stochastically) more integration than others, and likewise, some tasks such as coordinating skeletal muscle plans *require* more integration (Morsella 2005), so there will be strong patterns. Tononi thinks the richness of interconnectedness in cortical grids is particularly favorable for consciousness: "we have every reason to believe that, as regards the neural correlates of consciousness (NCC, e.g. here), the buck actually stops with some grid-like area … In sum, while the study of the neural correlates of consciousness is fraught with experimental and

---

[9] This would be valuable to chart in an individual brain, across individuals, across cultures, and across eras (e.g., Jaynes' 'bicameral mind' hypothesis).

interpretive difficulties, it seems clear that several topographically organized cortical maps likely contribute directly to the quality of our experience, and that manipulating such maps alters our consciousness." (Tononi 2014)

A very counter-intuitive implication of IIT is that if we slowly alter the integration of a system, we can come across discrete thresholds resulting in a sudden shift in where consciousness is occurring. E.g., if we slowly decrease the brain's inter-hemispherical integration, there will be a point where the brain's consciousness will split in two. Or if we gradually link two brains together, there will be a sudden threshold where the Φ of the combined system is greater than either Φs of the individual brains, and the two separate consciousnesses will suddenly combine into one. The math of IIT implies there will always be this sort of a 'competition' between different scales of a system to determine where the largest amount of Φ resides (and thus which scale 'counts' for consciousness).

IIT deals with identifying the *magnitude* (Φ) and *structure* of phenomenology. It leaves the *dynamical evolution* of these structures, and how these structures inform *behavior*, for others to fill in the blanks, and research here is just starting.

Finally, nobody- including Tononi- knows how big of a real-world dataset consciousness involves under IIT. E.g., is the average human-experience MIP billions of nodes? Orders of magnitude larger than that, given that 'the connectome' is a leaky level of abstraction? Or just a few thousand (some tiny subset of neurons deep in the thalamus or claustrum which actually 'count' for consciousness due to having a particularly high Φ and integration falling off quickly with causal distance? How many 'bits' are needed to represent human-like phenomenology under IIT? Bytes, Kilobytes, or terabytes? And how much does this vary from moment-to-moment?

How IIT and valence relate: As noted above, IIT aims to construct a mathematical object isomorphic to a system's phenomenology. Valence (how pleasant it is to be a conscious experience) is a subset of phenomenology. This implies that insofar as IIT has a valid goal, reverse-engineering valence is simply a matter of figuring out *how* valence is encoded within this mathematical object.

In short, IIT is currently a very *interesting* theory in this space that's generated a lot of buzz, and it seems likely that any alternatives must necessarily use many of the same sorts of assumptions, definitions, and techniques. It's also currently pretty much the only game in town for truly quantitative theories of consciousness. However, it also has vocal critics. Section IV will summarize and organize the criticisms levied against IIT.

IV. Critiques of IIT

IIT was the subject of a recent back-and-forth discussion (Aaronson 2014a) between Scott Aaronson, one of the world's foremost experts on computational complexity theory, Virgil Griffith, who recently obtained his PhD studying IIT under Christof Koch, David Chalmers, the philosopher who has coined much of the terminology around 'psychophysical laws', and Giulio Tononi, the theorist originally behind IIT. This back-and-forth discussion was both quantitative and qualitative, and is probably both the best 'gentle introduction' to IIT, and the grittiest pull-no-punches spotlight on its flaws. The critiques levied against IIT fell into three general bins:

Objection 1: IIT's math may not be correct.
Most neuroscientists seem to agree that a system having a high integration is probably *necessary* for consciousness, but it may not be *sufficient*. Furthermore, there are questions about whether IIT uses the correct methodology to calculate integration. Two concerns here stood out:

Objection 1.1: IIT's math is at times idiosyncratic and sloppy:

- Aaronson and Griffith both note that "a lack of mathematical clarity in the definition of Φ is a 'major problem in the IIT literature,'" and that "IIT needs more mathematically inclined people at its helm." They agree "'110%' that the lack of a derivation of the form of Φ from IIT's axioms is 'a pothole in the theory,'" and that "the current prescriptions for computing Φ contain many unjustified idiosyncrasies."
- Aaronson is particularly uneasy that "None of the papers I read—including the ones Giulio linked to in his response essay—contained anything that looked to me like a derivation of Φ. Instead, there was general discussion of the postulates, and then Φ just sort of appeared at some point. Furthermore, given the many idiosyncrasies of Φ—the minimization over all bipartite (why just bipartite? why not tripartite?) decompositions of the system, the need for normalization (or something else in version 3.0) to deal with highly-unbalanced partitions—it would be quite a surprise were it possible to derive its specific form from postulates of such generality." (Note: Aaronson was speaking of IIT 2.0; IIT 3.0 removes the need for normalization.)
- Griffith is clear that the mathematical formula for Φ, and the postulates it's nominally based on, have been changing in each revision. The way IIT has addressed time has also substantially evolved: "phi-2004 has no notion of time, phi-2008 looks "backwards" in time, and phi-2014 looks both backwards and forwards." A rapidly-changing formula may be a sign of healthy theoretical development, but it doesn't necessarily inspire confidence that the most recent revision expresses an eternal truth of nature.
- Griffith suggests that a good method to improve IIT's mathematical foundations "would be to replace the jury-rigged Earth-Mover's-Distance in phi-2014 with something from Grothendieck topology."

Objection 1.2: IIT's axioms may be incomplete:
- First, *IIT's axioms may be incomplete*: Griffith echoes a common refrain when he notes that, "As-is, there has been no argument for why the existing axioms of differentiation, integration, and exclusion fully exhaust the phenomological properties requiring explanation." I.e., IIT may constitute a *necessary* but not *sufficient* condition for consciousness. Still another way to phrase this is Michael Cerullo's notion that IIT is a theory of "protoconsciousness" instead of consciousness (Cerullo 2015), or that it doesn't capture all of what we want to speak of about the phenomenon of consciousness. Tononi seems to agree that it's a valid concern: "Nobody can be sure, certainly not me, that those [five] are all the axioms you need- or, for that matter it could even be, that there are some extra axioms that we don't need. But that I very much doubt." (Tononi and Albantakis 2014)
- Second, *IIT's algorithm could be incorrect*: some of the specific choices involved in the math IIT uses to construct its geometric figure (e.g., how 'integration' is formalized) may end up being empirically incorrect. Indeed, Aaronson identifies a simple-to-define mathematical structure called an "expander graph" which, according to the math used to calculate Φ, would produce *much more* consciousness than a human brain. Clearly, a good theory should sometimes correspond with our intuitions, and other times challenge them, but Aaronson is troubled by how easy it is to define something which would have lots of consciousness (Φ) but no behavior we would classify as 'intelligent'. (Tononi notes that Aaronson's 'expander graph' would need to be physically built to create these high levels of Φ, which would be tougher to pull off than it sounds, and this difficulty may make this example slightly more intuitively palatable.)

Objection 2: IIT is troublingly unclear on precisely what to use as its input.
In essence, there are many different ways IIT 3.0 could apply to a given physical system, and IIT is either ambiguous or arbitrary on how to choose between them. The key point of contention is Tononi's assertion that "elements may contribute to experience if-and-only-if they have the spatial grain (& temporal grain and state) associated with a maximum of Φ" (Tononi and Albantakis 2014) - i.e., that qualia are generated from whichever level of detail which maximizes integration. This is very clever, since it allows IIT to apply to neurons instead of single molecules, yet it's also quite maddening, since it punts on questions of what its ontological primitives really *are*.

The main uncertainties with IIT's input seem three-fold:
Objection 2.1: IIT's input is probably going to be something like a connectome, but there's a cloud of empirical uncertainty with this:

- Aaronson notes that we don't know the proper level of details at which to apply IIT: "The first difficulty is that we don't know the detailed interconnection network of the human brain. The second difficulty is that it's not even clear what we should define that network to be: for example, as a crude first attempt, should we assign a Boolean variable to each neuron, which equals 1 if the neuron is currently firing and 0 if it's not firing, and let f be the function that updates those variables over a timescale of, say, a millisecond? What other variables do we need—firing rates, internal states of the neurons, neurotransmitter levels?"
- … But even if we could build a realistically-detailed connectome, it's unclear whether the connectome would be *sufficient* for defining the-brain-as-conscious-system. Clearly the lion's share of functional causality seems transmitted by synaptic activity, but it would be surprising if hundreds of millions of years of evolution hasn't prepared our brains to use some surprising communication back-channels which aren't included in conventional connectome maps. E.g., a full causal diagram might need to take into account chemical gradients, glial cells, and EM/quantum stuff, among other things, which would take us very far from a crisp, high-level connectome.
- There's some progress by the Tsuchiya Lab on finding "measures of integrated information that can be applied to real neural recording data" (Oizumi et al. 2016), but this is merely a more-easily-computable *proxy* for IIT and is even less rigorous (since it doesn't use all of IIT's axioms).

Objection 2.2: IIT isn't clear about what its fundamental primitives are, or how to deal with different levels of abstraction, or how it fits into other physical theories:

- Even if we had a *fully comprehensive* map of causality in the brain, Tononi isn't clear on how to actually apply IIT. I.e., what are the nodes, and what are the vertices in IIT's input? How does IIT apply to a tiny, toy system, one where quantum effects may be significant? Tononi has never actually given a breakdown of how he thinks IIT applies to a real-world example, perhaps because the computational state of neurons is an inherently vague property (see Appendix C).
- A particularly thorny mechanic of IIT is the assertion that "elements may contribute to experience if-and-only-if they have the spatial grain associated with a maximum of Φ" and that we can basically ignore spatial grains that involve a low Φ. It's thorny because *it assumes that a* spatial *grain is a well-defined thing*- and it's unclear whether Tononi intends this to mean the *level of abstraction* (for example, quarks or neurons) that matters is the one which maximizes Φ.
- Even Tononi and his collaborators get tripped up on how this plays out empirically: in interviews, Cristof Koch notes, "I am a functionalist when it comes to consciousness. As long as we can reproduce the [same kind of] relevant relationships among all the relevant neurons in the brain, I think we will have recreated consciousness." (Koch 2015) Meanwhile, (Tononi and Koch 2015) argue that "in sharp contrast to widespread functionalist beliefs, IIT implies that digital computers, even if their behaviour were to be functionally equivalent to ours, and even if they were to run faithful simulations of the human brain, would experience next to nothing." Clarification on how IIT would apply to brain emulations & simulations, and to actual physical systems- preferably involving calculations on real examples- would be hugely illuminating and is sorely needed.

Objection 2.3: Some of IIT's metaphysics seem arbitrary. Specifically: more recent versions of IIT endorse an "anti-nesting principle", which prevents a system like the brain from generating a combinatorial explosion of consciousnesses. However, this principle seems inelegant and arbitrary:

- Eric Schwitzgebel notes that, according to this anti-nesting principle,
"A conscious entity cannot contain another conscious entity as a part. Tononi suggests that whenever one information-integrated system is nested in another, consciousness will exist only in the system with this highest degree of informational integration. Tononi defends this principle by appeal to Occam's razor, with intuitive support from the apparent absurdity of supposing that a third group consciousness could emerge from two people talking. … [but] Tononi's anti-nesting principle compromises the elegance of his earlier view … [and] has some odd consequences. For example, it implies that if an ultra-tiny conscious organism were somehow to become incorporated into your brain, you would suddenly be rendered nonconscious, despite the fact that all your behavior, including self-reports of consciousness, might remain the same. … Tononi's anti-nesting principle seems only to swap one set of counterintuitive implications for another, in the process

abandoning general, broadly appealing materialist principles – the sort of principles that suggest that beings broadly similar in their behavior, self-reports, functional sophistication, and evolutionary history should not differ radically with respect to the presence or absence of consciousness." (Schwitzgebel 2012b)

This 'anti-nesting' issue gets especially messy when combined with the issue of spatial grain, making it deeply unclear under exactly which conditions a given element is "spoken for" and cannot contribute to another complex. I.e., if a neuron is part of a connectome-scale complex, can some of the neuron's proteins or sub-atomic particles be a part of another nano-scale complex? IIT is silent here.

Objection 3: Tononi & Koch give little guidance for interpreting IIT's output.

Objection 3.1: IIT generates a very complicated data structure yet hardly says anything about what it means:
- As noted above, IIT suggests that the height of the geometric figure it generates, or Φ, corresponds to the degree to which the system is conscious. But no further guesses are offered, nor heuristics to generate them. (Balduzzi and Tononi 2009) offer some hypothetical mechanisms for how input to the visual system might correspond with IIT's phenomenology, but these are limited to very simple, toy systems. IIT is *nominally* about "PHP4"- which should tell us *everything* about a conscious experience- but in *reality* only addresses PHP3.5, or *how* conscious a system is.

Objection 3.2: IIT seems perilously *close to untestable.*
- IIT's predictions are only testable in circumstantial ways, and when IIT and our intuitions diverge, it's unclear which one should win. IIT wants to become the gold standard for consciousness, but how do we validate the gold standard?
- If Tononi et al. *did* give more guidance for interpreting the output- e.g., if IIT had a *rich set* of predictions, rather than a single prediction of how conscious a system is- it would give us a lot more angles by which to test, try to falsify, and improve IIT. As-is, however, IIT suffers from very loose feedback loops, which discourages investment in IIT.

<u>Aaronson's verdict</u>: "In my opinion, the fact that Integrated Information Theory is wrong—demonstrably wrong, for reasons that go to its core—puts it in something like the top 2% of all mathematical theories of consciousness ever proposed. Almost all competing theories of consciousness, it seems to me, have been so vague, fluffy, and malleable that they can only **aspire** to wrongness."

<u>Chalmers' verdict</u>: "Right now it's one of the few candidate partial answers that are formulated with a reasonable degree of precision. Of course as your discussion suggests, that precision makes it open to potential counterexamples. … In any case, at least formulating reasonably precise principles like this helps brings the study of consciousness into the domain of theories and refutations."

<u>Griffith's verdict</u>: "To your question "Is IIT valid?", the short answer is "Yes, with caveats." and "Probably not.", depending on the aspect of IIT under consideration. That said, IIT is currently *the* leading theory of consciousness. The prominent competitors are: Orch-OR, which isn't taken seriously due to (Tegmark 2000) on how quickly decoherence happens in the brain] and Global Workspace Theory, which is regularly seen as too qualitative to directly refute."

A window into Tononi's mind:
The dust may take a while to settle. I attended a small group discussion with Tononi at UC Berkeley, and the following is Tononi's 'felt sense' about some common criticisms:

- First, Aaronson's example of a 'dumb' grid system that nonetheless would have a very large Φ simply calls the question: how closely should we expect a theory of consciousness to match our intuitions in evolutionarily novel contexts? Tononi thinks we should expect some surprises, especially as we head into the computer era, and that intelligence and consciousness may not be as synonymous as Aaronson thinks. I.e., most of Aaronson's concerns involve IIT violating Aaronson's intuitions on consciousness, but as Eric Schwitzgebel notes, "Common sense is incoherent in matters of metaphysics. There's no way to develop an ambitious, broad-ranging, self-consistent metaphysical system without doing serious violence to common sense somewhere. It's just impossible. Since common sense is an inconsistent system, you can't respect it all. Every metaphysician will have to violate it somewhere." (Schwitzgebel 2012a)

- Tononi seemed frustrated that "people usually ignore the axioms, but they are the heart" (Tononi 2016); whenever critiques don't accept that IIT is at core a *phenomenological* theory, he thinks they miss something important.

- As noted above, Tononi has argued that "in sharp contrast to widespread functionalist beliefs, IIT implies that digital computers, even if their behaviour were to be functionally equivalent to ours, and even if they were to run faithful simulations of the human brain, would experience next to nothing." (Tononi and Koch 2015). However, he hasn't actually published much on *why* he thinks this. When pressed on this, he justified this assertion by reference to IIT's axiom of exclusion- this axiom effectively prevents 'double counting' a physical element to be part of multiple virtual elements, and when he ran a simple neural simulation on a simple microprocessor and looked at what the hardware was actually doing, a lot of the "virtual neurons" were being run on the same logic gates (in particular, all virtual neurons extensively share the logic gates which run the processor clock). Thus, the virtual neurons don't exist in the same causal clump ("cause-effect repertoire") like they do in a real brain. His conclusion was that there might be small fragments of consciousness scattered around a digital computer, but he's confident that 'virtual neurons' emulated on a Von Neumann system wouldn't produce their original qualia.

Finally, Tononi was emphatic that actual empirical measurements of Φ are really hard. Do things a little bit wrong, and you get garbage results.

V. Alternative versions of IIT: Perceptronium and FIIH

Section IV noted that while IIT is the most mature and predictive quantitative theory of consciousness we have, it also suffers from severe flaws. Others have been working on addressing these flaws by taking IIT's core insight that integration is fundamental to consciousness and 'porting' it to the language of physics. No such efforts are yet as formalized as IIT is, but the most notable here are Max Tegmark's "Perceptronium" and Adam Barrett's "FIIH".

Tegmark's Perceptronium: Max Tegmark has his own 'flavor' of IIT he calls Perceptronium (Tegmark 2015), which is essentially an attempt to *reconstruct* a framework that functions like IIT, but is grounded in fundamental quantum interactions (as opposed to Tononi's focus on neural/graph systems).

Perceptronium can be thought of as the combination of two themes:

First, that any theory of consciousness should *apply unambiguously to physical reality*, which means it needs to apply to *quantum systems*. Tegmark's basic approach here is to look at various ways of combining interaction terms in the Hamiltonian (a matrix used by Quantum Mechanics to represent the energy state of the universe). He believes a way of combining these interaction terms can be found that essentially reconstructs IIT's notion of 'integrated information' in terms of fundamental physics.

Second, Tegmark attempts to formally link the problem IIT deals with, 'what sorts of interactions give rise to consciousness?', with the long-standing Quantum Factorization Problem, or 'why do we experience *certain* factorizations of Hilbert Space (e.g., 3d+1 Space), but not *other* factorizations (e.g., Fourier Space)?' Tegmark argues that the former problem is *prior* to the latter: "we need a criterion for identifying conscious observers, and then a prescription that determines which factorization each of them will perceive."

So how does Tegmark actually try to solve the problem? A common thread in Tegmark's research is to apply anthropic reasoning to questions of physics fine-tuning, and Perceptronium is no exception. His first step is to identify certain complexity conditions which seems necessary to allow consciousness, and he believes we should be able to use this to narrow down what sorts of factorizations of Hilbert Space could support these requirements: "In other words, if we find that useful consciousness can only exist given certain strict requirements on the quantum factorization, then this could explain why we perceive a factorization satisfying these requirements."

The six anthropic-themed principles Tegmark has identified:
- *Information principle*: A conscious system has substantial information storage capacity.
- *Dynamics principle*: A conscious system has substantial information processing capacity.
- *Independence principle*: A conscious system has substantial independence from the rest of the world.
- *Integration principle*: A conscious system cannot consist of nearly independent parts.
- *Autonomy principle*: A conscious system has substantial dynamics and independence.
- *Utility principle*: An evolved conscious system records mainly information that is useful for it.

Since we're interested in Perceptronium as a theory of consciousness, not as a solution to the Quantum Factorization Problem, further details here aren't critical for our purposes. What matters for *us* is that Perceptronium should be considered a substantial "fork" of IIT, replacing IIT's 'ontologically agnostic' functionalism with the requirement that the ontological primitives of the theory (i.e., its inputs) be well-defined physical entities or properties. However, it does have the same goal as IIT, i.e. to generate a mathematical object isomorphic to the qualia of a system.

Strengths of Perceptronium:
- The universe is made from quantum stuff, so a theory designed to apply unambiguously to quantum stuff makes sense, and would avoid a core problem facing IIT (e.g., the universe is made from quarks, not XOR-gates!);
- Tegmark's math is much more elegant than Tononi et al.'s;
- Tegmark's anthropic approach seems like an effective heuristic to guide our search toward productive areas, and may address Aaronson's "expander grid" critique of IIT;
- By linking the problem of consciousness with the Quantum Factorization Problem, Tegmark gets some search space optimization 'for free', and also raises the stakes (if we *can* figure out one problem, the other becomes much more tractable).

Weaknesses of Perceptronium:
- Perceptronium is not fully formalized: it's merely a collection of *key considerations* of how to approach the consciousness/factorization problem. As such, it's less powerful & less legible than IIT;
- Perceptronium only addresses "PHP3.5" - *how* conscious systems are. It does not address PHP4, describing *which* conscious experiences a system is having;
- As Michael Cerullo notes, the attempt to add *functional* constraints on which systems are conscious can introduce pesky ambiguities: Perceptronium starts out trying to be *less* ambiguous than IIT by grounding itself in quantum interactions, yet "[u]nlike other states of matter, the properties of perceptronium are not physical properties but instead properties that depend on an interpretation of the arrangement of the matter as information." (M. Cerullo 2016) However, if Tegmark intends his six principles only as leaky-but-generative heuristics, this objection seems manageable;
- Tononi justifies looking for consciousness at the neural scales which seem relevant for consciousness via his notion that "elements may contribute to experience iff they have the spatial and temporal grain associated with a maximum of Φ"- and the connectome probably *is* the spatial grain that maximizes Φ. But how does Perceptronium, which deals with fundamental physics at tiny scales, get there?

The first two flaws are simply a factor of Perceptronium being a young theory; the third may or may not turn out to be significant, depending on the way Tegmark moves forward with formalizing Perceptronium, how exactly he applies the anthropic principle, and how he satisfices between the pressures to make something *in accordance with our intuitions about consciousness* vs *optimized for mathematical elegance and unambiguous application*. The fourth flaw, that Perceptronium doesn't seem to naturally apply at the right spatial and temporal grain, seems like the *core challenge* of the theory's approach (see Appendix E for some speculation on how this could be addressed). All that said, this seems like a very promising line of research.

Also of note, Tegmark has followed up with "Improved Measures of Integrated Information" (Tegmark 2016) which lists multiple methods (both existing and novel) by which to formalize integrated information in an IIT-style framework, each with slightly different tradeoffs, and goes on to offer (*staggeringly*) dramatic algorithmic speedups and approximations for computing some measures under certain cases.

		$\phi^{2.0}$	$\phi^{2.0'}$	$\phi^{2.0''}$	$\phi^{3.0}$	ϕ^M	ϕ^B	$\phi^M_{kk'}$	ϕ^{oakk}	ϕ^{opkk}	ϕ^{otsk}	ϕ^{ofuk}	ϕ^{nask}	ϕ^{mask}	ϕ^{xfkk}
Major	Always **non-negative**	y	y	y	y	y	N	y	y	y	y	y	y	y	y
	Always **finite** even for ∞-dimensional system	N	y	y	N	y	y	y	y	y	y	y	y	N	y	y
	Vanishes for **deterministic** system (drawback)	n	n	n	n	n	n	n	n	n	n	n	n	n	n	Y
	Vanishes for **separable** system	y	y	y	y	y	N	y	y	y	N	y	y	y	y
Minor	Vanishes for **afferent** system	y	y	y	y	N	N	N	y	N	N	N	y	y	N
	Vanishes for **efferent** system	y	y	y	y	N	N	N	N	y	N	N	N	N	N
	State-dependent	y	y	y	y	N	N	y	y	y	N	N	N	N	y
	Based on **symmetric** probability distance	N	N	N	y	N	N	n	N	N	N	N	N	N	N
	Intuitively **interpretatable**	2	2	2	2	2	0	2	2	2	0	1	0	0	0
	Computationally **tractable**	1	2	2	0	2	2	2	2	2	2	2	1	2	2

TABLE I: Properties of different integration measures. All but the third are desirable properties; capitalized N/Y (no/yes) indicate when an integration measure lacks a desirable property or has an undesirable one. The first four properties are generally agreed to be important, while the second set of four have been argued to be important by some authors. $\phi^M \equiv \phi^{otuk}$ and $\phi^M_{kk'} \equiv \phi^{ofkk}_{kk'}$.

Figure 3: Table I from Tegmark 2016. For definitions of each measure, see his Table II. However, it's important to note that the faster algorithms here are "mere" approximations, and they don't test for everything IIT does (causality, exclusion, spatio-temporal grain), merely integration.

Barrett's field integrated information hypothesis (FIIH): Adam Barrett takes a similar physics-centric tack with his version of IIT, but instead of focusing on quantum interactions, he focuses on reimagining IIT as a field theory. His *field integrated information hypothesis* (FIIH) argues that

(1) Quantum fields are fundamental entities in physics, and all particles can be understood as ripples in their specific type of field.
(2) Since they're so fundamental, it seems plausible that these fields could be carriers for consciousness.
(3) The gravity, strong, and weak nuclear fields probably can't support the complexity required for human consciousness: gravity's field is too simple to support structure since it only attracts, and disturbances in the other two don't propagate much further than the width of an atom's nucleus.
(4) However, we know the brain's neurons generate extensive, complex, and rapidly changing patterns in the electromagnetic field.
(5) Thus, we should look to the electromagnetic field as a possible 'carrier' to consciousness- with the amount of IIT-style integrated information in the EM field corresponding to *how much* consciousness.

Unfortunately, Barrett leaves the argument there without formalizing anything-- which is even less than Tegmark's Perceptronium offers. It also doesn't seem to have immediate empirical justification, since normal variation in nearby electromagnetic fields doesn't seem to influence or disrupt our consciousness even a little bit.[10] That said, the *a priori* argument is at least reasonable since quantum fields *are* fundamental, and this *style* of explanation is at least worth keeping an eye on, particularly in how it helps rule out certain areas of explanation space- e.g.,point (3).

---

[10] This isn't a fatal objection, since perhaps some abstract physical or mathematical justification could be made for why external interference from e.g., wireless routers and radio signals doesn't affect the internal geometry of integrated information in brain-scale EM fields. Or perhaps these *do* affect qualia, but don't trigger differences in our memories & self-reports. I discuss this a bit more in appendices C & E.

<u>In summary:</u> IIT is extremely promising approach for deriving the "data structure isomorphic to what it feels like to be a system" - but it's also deeply flawed or underdeveloped in certain details, and most neuroscientists don't see it as theoretically compelling or particularly usable *as-is*. Likewise, Perceptronium is an upcoming variant of IIT which may address some of these flaws, but it's still gestating and has its own challenges. FIIH attempts something similar, with a slightly different focus.

At any rate, I think there's an elegant way to synthesize everything I've written thus far and provide a firm foundation for further work on and around IIT. Section VI will explain how- and Section VIII will explore heuristics for how to extract interesting qualia (like valence) from IIT's output.

VI. Summary and synthesis: eight problems for a new science of consciousness

The best proximate solution for improving IIT would involve locking Tononi, Koch, Aaronson, Griffith, Tegmark, and maybe David Spivak (a leading expert on Grothendieck topology) in a room, and not letting them out until everybody's satisfied with the math. But I actually think there's another option that's much simpler, more effective in the long-term, and less likely to lead to police reports.

Essentially, IIT needs to address three classes of criticism: its math may be wrong, it's vague on what its inputs are, and it's vague on what its output means. I suggest that we leverage these criticisms to clarify that "solving consciousness" involves *three distinct core tasks*:
(1) <u>Metaphysics: what *matters* for consciousness?</u> How do we abstract the architecture (e.g., a network logic or circuit diagram) of a conscious system? I.e., what elements and processes in the physical world are necessary and sufficient for describing its qualia, and at which levels of abstraction should these things be defined? -- *IIT says very little about this.*
(2) <u>Math: *how* does this matter for consciousness?</u> How do we reorganize this causal map into a data structure isomorphic to that system's qualia? -- *this is the core of what IIT is attempting to do.*
(3) <u>Interpretation: How do we figure out what the math *means*?</u> I.e., given a "data structure isomorphic to that system's qualia", how do we map interesting properties of this structure to interesting stuff in the qualia domain, and vice-versa? — *for instance, what property does valence correspond to?*

These steps seem both *necessary* and *sufficient*: any full theory of consciousness will have to do these things, and if we can give a rigorous answer to all three, we'll have a complete theory of consciousness.

A rigorous "theory of consciousness" involves three separate tasks:

Task 1: Abstraction. How do we translate from a *physical system* to a *logical system* (i.e., how do we measure & diagram the relationships between what's relevant for consciousness, and figure out which details can we safely discard)?

→ Metaphysics of consciousness

Physical system (neurons, synapses, support cells, EM/chemical communication, quantum stuff, etc. all jumbled together and of uncertain significance.)

Task 2: Restructuring. How do we restructure this *abstraction* (essentially a disorganized wiring diagram) into a data structure whose structure is isomorphic to the phenomenology of the system? (Example: IIT)

→ Mathematics of consciousness

Logical Diagram (physical processes/nodes/information flows relevant for consciousness preserved and abstracted into a logical diagram, with no further post-processing)

Task 3: Interpretation. How do we figure out which properties of this data-structure-isomorphic-to-consciousness correspond to things we're interested in?

→ Interpretation/ translation of mathematical object

Mathematical Object (elements of logical system reorganized into a mathematical object whose structure is isomorphic to the system's phenomenological experience)

Meaning (human-level facts about the qualia of the system, e.g., how conscious a system is, how pleasant vs unpleasant the conscious experience is, whether it's experiencing redness or the smell of cinnamon, etc

Figure 4: a quantitative solution to consciousness involves three sorts of tasks.

Synthesis: Eight Problems for a New Science of Consciousness

The three steps described above seem like clean abstractions- firm hand-holds we can use when grappling with the problem of consciousness. But within each step we can identify further, more granular subtasks:

Step 1 (metaphysics) breaks down into two subproblems:
1. **The Reality Mapping Problem:** how do we choose a formal ontology for consciousness which can map unambiguously to reality?
2. **The Substrate Problem:** which subset of objects & processes in our chosen ontology 'count' toward consciousness?

Step 2 (math) breaks down into four subproblems:
1. **The Boundary (Binding[11]) Problem:** how do we determine the correct boundaries of a conscious system in a principled way?
2. **The Scale Problem:** how do we bridge the scale gap from our initial ontology (e.g., the Standard Model, string theory, individual computations, etc) to the spatial and temporal scales relevant to consciousness?
3. **The Topology of Information Problem[12]:** how do we restructure the information inside the boundary of the conscious system into a mathematical object isomorphic to the system's phenomenology?
4. **The State Space[13] Problem:** what is 'Qualia space'? - I.e., which precise mathematical object does the mathematical object isomorphic to a system's qualia live in? What are its structures/properties?

Step 3 (interpretation) breaks down into two subproblems:
1. **The Vocabulary Problem:** what are some guiding principles for how to improve our language about phenomenology so as to "carve reality at the joints"?
2. **The Translation Problem:** given a mathematical object isomorphic to a system's phenomenology, how do we populate a translation list between its mathematical properties and the part of phenomenology each property or pattern corresponds to?

My claim is that these eight sub-problems are necessary to solve consciousness, and in aggregate, may be sufficient.

---

[11] Generally philosophers refer to this as the 'Binding Problem'. Both ways of phrasing this problem are logically identical, but each has a slightly different focus: 'binding problem' implies that we should look for a property which is true throughout a given conscious system, whereas 'boundary problem' implies we should look for what changes beyond the boundary of a conscious system.
[12] This roughly maps to Chalmers' 'combination problem' ("how do the experiences of fundamental physical entities such as quarks and photons combine to yield the familiar sort of human conscious experience that we know and love?") but his terminology & subproblems also overlaps with the Boundary, Scale, and Topology of Information problems.
[13] More colloquially, we can refer to this as The Container Problem.

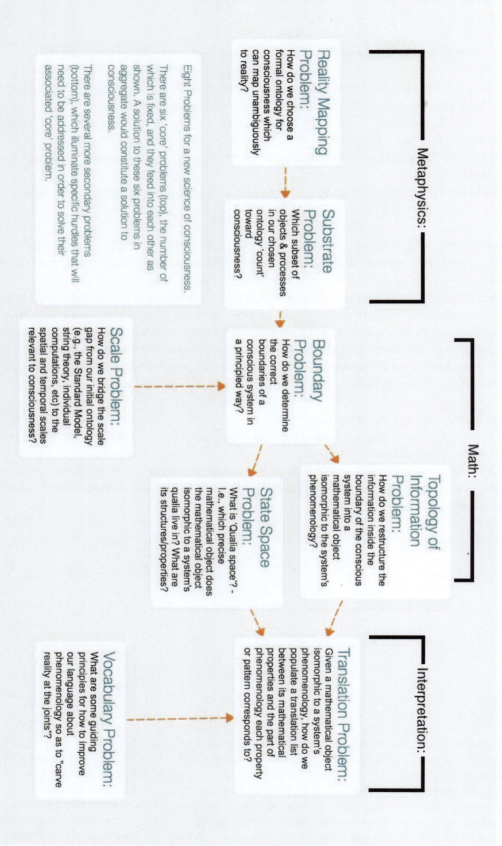

Figure 5: Unpacking 'The Problem of Consciousness' into discrete sub-problems.

	IIT3.0	Perceptronium	Orch-OR	My hypotheses (later in paper)	Other common Φ measures	Aaronson's decoherence hypothesis (1,2)	Functionalism	(McFadden/Qiu/Barrett) EM theories of consciousness	David Pearce's quantum binding hypothesis
Reality Mapping Problem	N?	Y	Y		N?	Y	N?	Y	Y
Substrate Problem	Y	partial	Y		Y	partial	partial	Y	Y
Boundary Problem	Y	?	Y		Y	?	?	?	Y
Scale Problem	Y	?	Y		Y	?	Y	Y	?
Topology of Information Problem	Y	?	?		?	?	?	?	?
State Space Problem	partial	?	?	partial	?	?	?	?	partial
Vocabulary Problem				partial					
Translation Problem				partial					
Makes falsifiable predictions	Y?	?	Y	Y	Y?	?	N	Y?	Y

Table 1: Table of problems and whether popular consciousness theories address them.
Legend: "Y" signifies that a theory explicitly attempts a problem; "?" signifies that it doesn't, but might be extended to do so; "N" signifies that it dismisses a problem. Color represents how much supporting literature there seems to be on whether a theory has (or *could have*) a plausible approach on a given problem (Green>Blue>Red).

Several things follow from this:

First, it's clear that the options for how to approach Step 2 (the math) are somewhat constrained and informed by the choices made in Step 1 (choice of ontology). However, Step 3 (interpretation) is largely or wholly orthogonal, and can be approached separately no matter how a "mathematical object isomorphic to a system's phenomenology" is generated. This should allow us to move from a "cathedral" or "silo" model of consciousness research, to a more distributed "bazaar", mixing and matching different assumptions and techniques.

Second, we can see why IIT is so impressive: using only 1-2 mechanics it can address all of Step 2's subproblems. However, we also see why Tegmark is interested in grounding IIT in the ontology of physics: right now IIT ignores nuances of the Reality Mapping Problem, which implies that application of IIT to real physical systems will always have a cloud of ambiguity around it.

Part II - Valence

VII. Three principles for a mathematical derivation of valence

We've covered a lot of ground with the above literature reviews, and synthesizing a new framework for understanding consciousness research. But we haven't yet fulfilled the promise about valence made in Section II- to offer a *rigorous, crisp,* and relatively *simple* hypothesis about valence. This is the goal of Part II.

Drawing from the framework in Section VI, I offer three principles to frame this problem:

1. Qualia Formalism: *for any given conscious experience, there exists- in principle- a mathematical object isomorphic to its phenomenology.*
-->This is a formal way of saying that consciousness is in principle quantifiable- much as electromagnetism, or the square root of nine is quantifiable. I.e. IIT's goal, to generate such a mathematical object, is a valid one.

2. Qualia Structuralism: *this mathematical object has a rich set of formal structures.*
-->Based on the regularities & invariances in phenomenology, it seems safe to say that qualia has a non-trivial amount of structure. It likely exhibits *connectedness* (i.e., it's a unified whole, not the union of multiple disjoint sets), and *compactness*, and so we can speak of qualia as having a *topology*.

More speculatively, based on the following:
(a) IIT's output format is data in a vector space,
(b) Modern physics models reality as a wave function within Hilbert Space, which has substantial structure,
(c) Components of phenomenology such as color behave as vectors (Feynman 1965), and
(d) Spatial awareness is explicitly geometric,
... I propose that Qualia space also likely satisfies the requirements of being a metric space, and we can speak of qualia as having a *geometry*.[14]

Mathematical structures are <u>important</u>, since *the more formal structures a mathematical object has, the more elegantly we can speak about patterns within it, and the closer our words can get to "carving reality at the joints".*

3. Valence Realism: *valence is a crisp phenomenon of conscious states upon which we can apply a measure.*[15]
-->I.e. some experiences do feel holistically *better* than others, and (*in principle*) we can associate a value to this. Furthermore, to combine (2) and (3), this pleasantness could be encoded into the mathematical object isomorphic to the experience in an *efficient* way. I.e., we should look for a *concise equation,* not an infinitely-large *lookup table* for valence.

-->Assumptions I *do not* require:
- That IIT is anywhere close to correct in *general*;
- That IIT is close to correct with regard to having the right input, or mathematical process;
- That integration is the key type of complexity causing consciousness;

---

[14] Technically speaking, this is a stronger assumption than my hypothesis about valence requires- all my load-bearing distinctions can also be applied to 'mere' graphs as well- but I think it's a fairly safe assumption and it makes the argument much easier to follow intuitively. See Appendix D for more. That said, I suspect Qualia space has much more structure than this- I suspect it could be a Hilbert space.

[15] Thanks to David Pearce for making the intuitive & philosophical case that valence (hedonic tone, as he puts it) is 'real'.

- That understanding the quantum effects occurring in the brain will be important, or will be unimportant, to modeling consciousness;
- That valence is strictly one-dimensional;
- That any specific metaphysics of consciousness (physicalism, panpsychism, functionalism, dualism, etc) is true[16];
- That this isomorphic data structure is empirically measurable or finite.

Obviously, if IIT is pretty close to correct it simplifies many things, but it's important to note that I'm agnostic on almost all particulars of IIT. I bring IIT in as the most established and critiqued example of how we may plausibly construct a "data structure isomorphic to a system's phenomenology", but I don't *need* it for the balance of this paper. Indeed, if you have a favorite alternative or pet hypothesis as to how to generate such a data structure, I encourage you to mentally replace mentions of IIT with that as we continue.

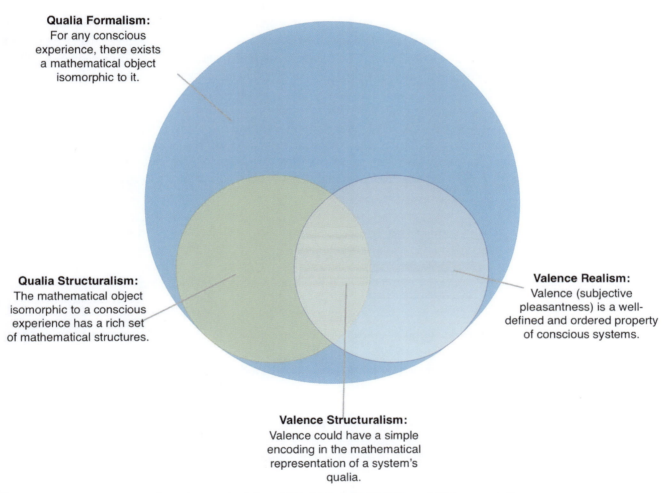

Figure 6: A Venn Diagram of my three principles. 1&2, 1&3, and 1&2&3 are valid permutations.

---

[16] The balance of my paper is agnostic on how to get to this interpretation step, but my appendices assume physicalism is correct. See Appendix C for more.

I believe my three principles are all *necessary* for a satisfying solution to valence (and the first two are necessary for any satisfying solution to consciousness):

Considering the inverses:

If *Qualia Formalism* is false, then consciousness is not quantifiable, and there exists no formal knowledge about consciousness to discover. But if the history of science is any guide, we don't live in a universe where phenomena are intrinsically unquantifiable- rather, we just haven't been able to crisply quantify consciousness *yet*.

If *Qualia Structuralism* is false and Qualia space has no meaningful structure to discover and generalize from, then most sorts of knowledge about qualia (such as which experiences feel better than others) will likely be forever beyond our empirical grasp. I.e., if Qualia space lacks structure, there will exist no elegant heuristics or principles for interpreting what a mathematical object isomorphic to a conscious experience *means*. But this doesn't seem to match the story from affective neuroscience, nor from our everyday experience: we have *plenty* of evidence for patterns, regularities, and invariances in phenomenological experiences. Moreover, our informal, intuitive models for predicting our future qualia are generally *very good*. This implies our brains have figured out some simple rules-of-thumb for how qualia is structured, and so qualia does *have* substantial mathematical structure, even if our formal models lag behind.

If *Valence Realism* is false, then we really can't say very much about ethics, normativity, or valence with any confidence, *ever*. But this seems to violate the revealed preferences of the vast majority of people: we sure *behave* as some experiences are objectively superior to others, at arbitrarily-fine levels of distinction. It may be *very difficult* to put an objective valence on a given experience, but in practice we don't behave as if this valence doesn't *exist*.

We could spend thousands of words further fleshing out, contextualizing, and defending this metaphysical framework, and I think there would be value in this. However, as a general rule, I think <u>one should only focus on metaphysics if one cannot argue falsifiable predictions</u>-- and I think my framework *can* build falsifiable predictions. So for now, let us take these three principles as given, and see what we can build from them.

VIII. Distinctions in qualia: charting the explanation space for valence

Sections II-III made the claim that we need a bottom-up quantitative theory *like* IIT in order to successfully reverse-engineer valence, Section VI suggested some core problems & issues theories like IIT will need to address, and Section VII proposed three principles for interpreting IIT-style output:
(1) we should think of qualia as having a mathematical representation,
(2) this mathematical representation has a topology and probably a geometry, and perhaps more structure, and
(3) valence is real; some things do feel better than others, and we should try to explain why in terms of qualia's mathematical representation.

But what does this get us? Specifically, how does assuming these three things get us any closer to solving valence if we *don't have an actual, validated dataset ("data structure isomorphic to the phenomenology") from *any* system, much less a real brain*?

It actually helps a *surprising amount,* since an *isomorphism* between a structured (e.g., topological, geometric) space and qualia implies that *any clean or useful distinction we can make in one realm automatically applies in the other realm as well*. And if we can explore what kinds of distinctions in qualia we can make, we can start to chart the explanation space for valence (what 'kind' of answer it will be).

I propose the following four distinctions which depend on only a very small amount of mathematical structure inherent in qualia space, which should apply equally to qualia and to qualia's mathematical representation:

- <u>Global vs local</u>;
- <u>Simple vs complex</u>;
- <u>Atomic vs composite</u>;
- <u>Intuitively important vs intuitively trivial</u>.

Global vs local:

Some qualia (such as the sensation of green) seem fairly localized. We should expect their mathematical representations in Qualia Space to be fairly local properties too.

Other qualia, however, seem to permeate all other sensations- these should correspond to *distributed* or *holographic* properties of our mathematical structure as a *whole*.

My hypothesis is that valence is a *global* property, since a given mental state's valence is attached to every part of its phenomenology. I.e., pleasure[17] is not something that can be experienced distinctly or in isolation from other qualia (unlike, for instance, the sensations of 'redness' or 'a cat').[18]

Simple vs complex:

In short, if some quale corresponds to a basic/foundational topological property *of* the data structure, or is a small or highly compressible pattern *in* the data structure, it's simple; otherwise, it's complex. We can formalize just *how* simple something is in terms of its "Kolmogorov complexity"[19], or the shortest program necessary to specify it within, or derive it from, our data structure. E.g., the Kolmogorov complexity of the data structure isomorphic to the phenomenology of a human brain is likely gigantic, but the Kolmogorov complexity needed to *derive* Φ from this structure would be small enough to fit on a t-shirt. This also gives us a clear guide to whether some kind of qualia is a "natural kind": if something isn't a "natural kind" (e.g., "anger" or "joyfulness"), it'll necessarily have a large and/or ambiguous Kolmogorov complexity.

Valence doesn't seem to take much information to encode, and so it seems plausible that it could have a very low Kolmogorov complexity.

---

[17] Pleasure seems a little bit *more* unambiguously global than pain.
[18] It seems generally safe to say that *local* properties/qualia are often *representational*- that is, there's at least a rough correspondence between that qualia and something-in-the-world. For instance, if you're experiencing the qualia of a cat, chances are there's something with similar cat-like properties in your neighborhood of reality. *Global* properties of qualia, on the other hand, are less likely to be representational and thus less likely to reflect anything inherent about the world.
[19] The exact complexity measure we use is flexible; I mention Kolmogorov complexity because it's simple to describe and well-defined on most datasets. We may want another measure for simplicity of dynamics (thanks to Radhika Dirks for this clarification).

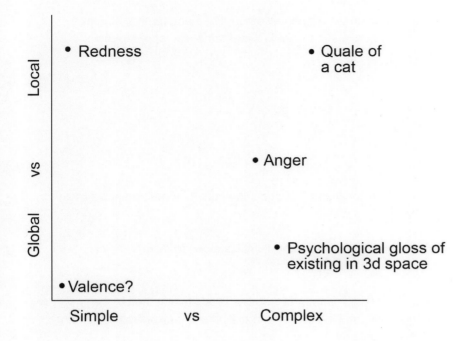

Figure 7: Estimated plot of various qualia along the global vs local, and simple vs complex axes.

Importantly, if some *quale* (such as valence) is highly global & simple, its *mathematical/geometric representation* will be as well.

Atomic vs composite:

We can make another distinction between <u>*atomic vs composite*</u> properties/qualia. My hypothesis is that valence is *atomic*, indivisible in a way that, e.g., post-modern angst or the quale of a cat aren't. (This is similar to but subtly different from the *simple vs complex* distinction.)

It seems plausible that how *universal* a quale seems will be a good indicator of how *atomic* it is. And valence seems uniquely universalizable- e.g., we can't know if the first alien species we meet will experience blue, taste, jealousy, etc. But it's probably safe to say that some of its experiences feel better than others- that it experiences valence.

Intuitively important vs intuitively trivial:

A rather fuzzy yet potentially very generative heuristic is that <u>*an isomorphism informally implies the existence of a rough correspondence between the most interesting elements of each data set.*</u> I.e., if we list the major/obvious/significant properties of a data-structure-isomorphic-to-phenomenology, these should correspond to things in the qualia domain of roughly the same "interestingness" rank (and vice versa!).

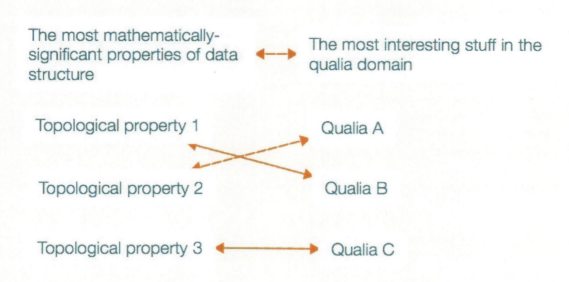

Figure 8: Properties ranked by intuitive 'interestingness' will <u>roughly</u> map to similarly-interesting things.

Obviously, there's a subjective element to 'interestingness' or 'importance' in both domains, and there are limitations on what we can say about properties of the data structure, since (1) we don't have an actual empirical example from IIT yet, and (2) IIT (or some future alternative) may change a great deal of the math before it gets things exactly right. But we *can* speak about interesting qualia, and about *general* geometric/topological properties which would be relevant to and important in *any* geometric/structured data (e.g., properties that mathematicians and deep learning algorithms would latch onto first), especially properties that should vary the *least* with regard to future IIT iterations (which would be properties that are *simple*, *global*, and *atomic*).

Valence seems like the *most* intuitively-interesting/important quale[20], so- as a rough heuristic- it should have a similarly-intuitively-interesting/important geometric counterpart. It's probably not some esoteric, technical, boring mathematical property- it's probably something that mathematicians would *notice*.

<u>Takeaways:</u> this section has suggested that we can get *surprising mileage* out of the hypothesis that there will exist a geometric data structure isomorphic to the phenomenology of a system, since if we can make a distinction in one domain (math or qualia), it will carry over into the other domain 'for free'. Given this, I put forth the hypothesis that valence may plausibly be a <u>*simple, global, atomic, and intuitively important property*</u> of both qualia and its mathematical representation.

Section IX will survey further reasons to believe valence is specifically a *simple*, *global*, and *atomic* property, and will also explore some heuristics intended to help us zero in on exactly *which* such property could correspond to valence.

---

[20] Chalmers coined the terms "Easy Problem of Consciousness" for how the brain processes information, and "Hard Problem of Consciousness" for why we're conscious at all. Perhaps we can call reverse-engineering valence the "Important Problem of Consciousness".

IX. Summary of heuristics for reverse-engineering the pattern for valence

Reverse-engineering the precise mathematical property that corresponds to valence may seem like finding a needle in a haystack, but I propose that it may be easier than it appears. Broadly speaking, I see six heuristics for zeroing in on valence:

- A. Structural distinctions in Qualia space (Section VIII);
- B. Empirical hints from affective neuroscience (Section I);
- C. *A priori* hints from phenomenology;
- D. Empirical hints from neurocomputational syntax;
- E. The *Non-adaptedness Principle*;
- F. Common patterns across physical formalisms (lessons from physics).

None of these heuristics *determine* the answer, but in aggregate they dramatically reduce the search space.

IX.A: Structural distinctions in Qualia space (Section VIII):
In the previous section, we noted that the following distinctions about qualia can be made:
- Global vs local;
- Simple vs complex;
- Atomic vs composite;
- Intuitively important vs intuitively trivial.

Valence plausibly corresponds to a *global, simple, atomic,* and *intuitively important* mathematical property.

IX.B: Empirical hints from affective neuroscience (Section I):
Our mathematical hypothesis for valence must be consistent with what we know from affective neuroscience. We can refer to Section I for more details, but a particularly important fact is that creating positive valence seems like a *centrally-coordinated* process, requiring hedonic regions-- whereas pain seems like a more distributed process that doesn't seem to require specialized circuitry to the same degree. We should look for a property that exhibits this imbalance.

We should also look for a property that can be *useful* in building brains, especially in the same way that pleasure and pain are used. I.e., if we were building a complex adaptive system via evolution, what sort of systemic property could we use as a foundation for reinforcement learning, value & salience detection and threat detection?

One specific remark here is that we seem to be "drawn to" pleasure, and "repelled from" pain. From a systems architecture perspective, this may be a hint that pleasure corresponds to a type of pattern that's easy to construct a very 'sticky' dynamic attractor for, and pain to a type of pattern that's easy to construct a dynamic repeller for.

IX.C: *A priori* hints from phenomenology:
It's dangerous to put too much weight on conclusions drawn from phenomenology, for the reasons mentioned in Section II: we have little reason to believe there's a clear mapping between the psychology of *how* we experience things and what *generates* our experience. However, it can offer some tentative hints.

(1) Very intense pain and very intense pleasure seem to be informationally/computationally sparse: the closer to either extreme the brain gets, the less room there seems to be for complexity.

(2) Most degradations of general function- sleep deprivation, hangovers, lethargic depression inflammation, interrupting loud noises, and in general most things that would intuitively increase entropy in the brain- seem to degrade the brain's ability to generate positive valence.

(3) Slightly less than two degrees of freedom seem necessary & sufficient to describe valence space (thus implying that valence is both fairly *simple* and *atomic*):

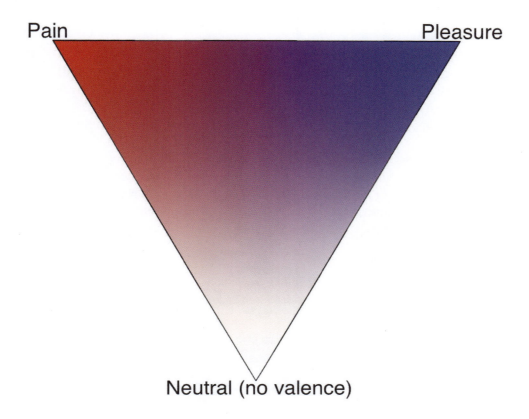

Figure 9: the triangle continuum of valence (from introspection).

IX.D: Hints from neurocomputational syntaxes:
Neuroscience doesn't give us any clear stories about what sort(s) of patterns cause valence, but there are some interesting hints scattered around in the context of neurocomputational syntax. Generally speaking, if we can get a feel for what sorts of information-theoretic things are going on during pleasure, it'll help guide us to the right area of the search space.

The brain seems to rely on a complex, overlapping hodgepodge of computational syntaxes, and neuroscience doesn't have a satisfyingly full accounting of what computational syntaxes the brain uses, let alone how they combine and interact, which limits what we can say here. However, a rule of thumb seems to be that pleasure seems to be often associated with *successful computations* in the brain, whereas unsuccessful computations (when the brain '*throws an exception*', in the parlance of computer programming) often feel unpleasant. By implication, *the type of data structure implied or generated by a successful computation may intrinsically feel good*, and vice-versa with unsuccessful computations. So -- what makes for a successful computation?

- Paul Smolensky's "Computational Harmony" is a multi-level neurocomputational syntax which applies especially in the natural-language processing (NLP) domain:
> "[Computational Harmony] is a connectionist well-formedness measure; it is maximized by μ-level spreading activation processes. At the M level, in the language domain, Harmony has a symbolic interpretation as an extension of the traditional linguistic notion of markedness (Battistella, 1990; Jakobson, 1962). A linguistic

> structure is called marked when it is relatively complex or in some sense defective; marked representations have lower Harmony and are thus avoided by the language-processing system." (Smolensky 2006)

… in short, Smolensky's model suggests that the organizing principle of successful neuro-linguistic computation is *simplicity* (->pleasure?), and our NLP systems avoid *needless complexity* (->pain?).

- Karl Friston's Free Energy model of brain dynamics comes to a roughly similar conclusion:
> "[A]ny self-organizing system that is at equilibrium with its environment must minimize its free energy. The principle is essentially a mathematical formulation of how adaptive systems (that is, biological agents, like animals or brains) resist a natural tendency to disorder. … In short, the long-term (distal) imperative — of maintaining states within physiological bounds — translates into a short-term (proximal) avoidance of surprise." (Friston 2010)

… in short, the brain will be organized around energy-efficient, 'elegant and accurate' computations which *minimize the entropic perturbation* (free energy) of the system in the long term. Positive valence can be modeled as "negative rate of change of free-energy over time" (Joffily and Coricelli 2013), whereas increasing amounts of free energy would produce negative valence. Other prediction-centric paradigms such as Predictive Error Minimization (Clark 2013; Seth 2013) and Compression Drive (Schmidhuber 2009) point to similar 'elegant order feels good; chaotic disorder feels bad' conclusions.

- The brain seems to deeply rely on phase-locking, rhythmic oscillations (Buzsaki 2006), and harmonics (Atasoy, Donnelly, and Pearson 2016), both of which exhibit a similar sort of elegant mathematical order.

- Leda Cosmides' work on motivation suggests we may be able to say that some types of important computation intrinsically feel bad:
> Why do we spend so much time and attention feeling: grief, anger, guilt and so forth? … What we've been pursuing is the idea that what generates these feelings is a layer of neuro-computational procedures and representations—what we're going to call internal regulatory variables—devices that compute them, and decision rules that these variables feed. And that these cause us to feel certain very specific motivations and value-specific outcomes and express certain kinds of behaviors, given certain inputs. (Cosmides 2011)

… in short, Cosmides argues that emotions like grief- or rather, processes like 'working through grief'- are actually computationally intensive, and the kind of computation involved with this sort of recalibration of internal regulatory variables seems to *intrinsically hurt*. Insofar as we can say things about what sorts of computations are causally related to these sorts of negative emotions and vice-versa, we may be able to say something about the computational syntax of valence.

As a provisional distillation of the circumstantial evidence here, I offer that the creation and maintenance of mathematically elegant patterns in the brain is associated with positive valence; the fracturing of existing elegant patterns with negative valence.

IX.E: The Non-adaptedness principle:
Finally: evolutionary psychology lets us roughly estimate how pleasurable a stimulus *should* be, given our evolutionary history, and we can compare this to how pleasurable the stimulus actually *is*. If we can find a stimulus where there's a large difference between these two quantities, it could be a hint of something interesting happening: some pattern "directly hacking into" the mental pattern which produces pleasure/pain.

I provisionally suggest the following as plausible outliers of this type:

Music is surprisingly pleasurable; auditory dissonance is surprisingly unpleasant. Clearly, music has many adaptive signaling & social bonding aspects (Storr 1992; Mcdermott and Hauser 2005)- yet if we subtract everything that could be considered signaling or social bonding (e.g., lyrics, performative aspects, social bonding & enjoyment), we're still left with something very emotionally powerful. However, this pleasantness can vanish abruptly- and even *reverse*- if dissonance is added.

Much more could be said here, but a few of the more interesting data points are:
- Pleasurable music tends to involve elegant structure when represented geometrically (Tymoczko 2006);
- Non-human animals don't seem to find human music pleasant (with some exceptions), but with knowledge of what pitch range and tempo their auditory systems are optimized to pay attention to, we've been able to *adapt* human music to get animals to prefer it over silence (Snowdon and Teie 2010).
- Results suggest that consonance is a primary factor in which sounds are pleasant vs unpleasant in 2- and 4-month-old infants (Trainor, Tsang, and Cheung 2002).
- Hearing two of our favorite songs at once doesn't feel better than just one; instead, it feels *significantly* worse.

More generally, it feels like music is a *particularly interesting* case study by which to pick apart the information-theoretic aspects of valence, and it seems plausible that evolution may have piggybacked on some fundamental law of qualia to produce the human preference for music. This should be most *obscured* with genres of music which focus on lyrics, social proof & social cohesion (e.g., pop music), and performative aspects, and *clearest* with genres of music which avoid these things (e.g., certain genres of classical music).

Abstract mathematics can be surprisingly pleasurable. To those mathematicians who can see them clearly, certain logical structures of abstract mathematics can seem starkly, and strikingly, beautiful. To some degree enjoyment of mathematical elegance must be a spandrel, pleasurable because it's been adaptive to value the ability to compress complexity... but pleasure does have to resolve to something, and this is an important data point. As Bertrand Russell puts it in The Study of Mathematics (Russell 1919):

> Mathematics, rightly viewed, possesses not only truth, but supreme beauty--a beauty cold and austere, like that of sculpture, without appeal to any part of our weaker nature, without the gorgeous trappings of painting or music, yet sublimely pure, and capable of a stern perfection such as only the greatest art can show. The true spirit of delight, the exaltation, the sense of being more than Man, which is the touchstone of the highest excellence, is to be found in mathematics as surely as in poetry.[21]

Flow states are surprisingly pleasurable. Getting lost in a task and entering flow tends to improve the experience. There are three possible implications here: first, that when a brain is successfully computing something, these successes feel good. Second, that time compression tends to feels good (or rather, it's associated with a relative improvement in valence). Third, and more speculatively, perhaps this second point loosely implies that *more pleasant brain states are more compressible*. (Large caveat: valence is not the only variable in play with regard to time perception- e.g., novelty is important as well.)

Cognitive dissonance and confusion are surprisingly unpleasant. In fact, 'dissonance' and 'pain' are often used as rough synonyms. Usually there's a messy range of valences associated with any given phenomenon- some people like it, some people don't. But I've never heard anyone say, "I felt cognitive dissonance and it felt *great.*"

IX.F: Common patterns across physical formalisms (lessons from physics)

---

[21] An important variable here is that not everyone is equally sensitive to environmental reward. My impression is that for most people, pleasure from the brain's natural reward systems tends to be much more reliable than trying to 'hack' it via exposure to whatever information-theoretic pattern corresponds to valence in conscious systems. I.e., most people don't bliss out on math because it's easy for them to find that same pleasure elsewhere. However, for e.g. high-AQ individuals who tend to be less sensitive to rewards in their social environments, we may predict relatively more effort spent seeking high-elegance mathematics & high-harmony music with no lyrics vs normal social pleasures.

If valence is a physical quantity- like charge, momentum, or curvature of spacetime- we should look at how physics represents other, similar quantities. Are there common patterns in physical formalisms? What mathematical tools and concepts have been successful elsewhere in describing the physical details of our universe?

Eugene Wigner has argued for the "unreasonable effectiveness of mathematics in the natural sciences" (E. P. Wigner 1960), and notes that the most successful physical formalisms are often the most starkly beautiful. (I will share my hypothesis and get back to this in the next section.)

X. A simple hypothesis about valence

To recap, the *general* heuristic from Section VIII was that valence may plausibly correspond to a *simple, atomic, global,* and *intuitively important* geometric property of a data structure isomorphic to phenomenology. The *specific* heuristics from Section IX surveyed hints from *a priori* phenomenology, hints from what we know of the brain's computational syntax, introduced the Non-adaptedness Principle, and noted the unreasonable effectiveness of beautiful mathematics in physics to suggest that the specific geometric property corresponding to pleasure should be something that involves some sort of *mathematically-interesting patterning, regularity, efficiency, elegance, and/or harmony*.

We don't have enough information to *formally deduce* which mathematical property these constraints indicate, yet in aggregate these constraints hugely reduce the search space, and also substantially point toward the following:

Given a mathematical object isomorphic to the qualia of a system, the mathematical property which corresponds to how pleasant it is to be that system is that object's <u>symmetry</u>.

<u>How do we quantify symmetry?</u>
In its most basic form, symmetry means invariance under transformations- i.e., for each symmetry something exhibits, there exists a type of transformation we could apply to it that effectively wouldn't do anything (e.g., rotating a square 90°). Frank Wilczek puts this as "change without change", and any mathematical object can have symmetries-- geometric figures, groups, and even equations.

But how do we formalize this and what do we want in a measure? Here are some variables that seem relevant:
1. How sensitive is the measure to small changes? E.g., if 1 of 100 elements of a maximally-symmetric object is moved with the intent to disrupt symmetry, will this decrease the measure by 1% or by 80%?
2. Likewise, how sensitive is the measure to partial symmetries? In any large dataset, the number of complete symmetries might be very low, but there might still be lots of partially-symmetrical order.
2.1. Should symmetry be measured holistically, or <u>should all parts of the mathematical object be evaluated for symmetry separately and/or in relation to each other, and then these quantities are aggregated together?</u>
3. How convergent is the measure with other measure of symmetry? I.e., does it reflect an idiosyncratic definition of symmetry?
4. How versatile is the measure? Does it apply to all mathematical objects? How does it handle fractal patterns?
5. Does it change much if the details of, e.g., how IIT constructs the space is updated? Does it fit with our best hypothesis on the State Space Problem?
6. How easy to compute is the measure?
7. How conceptually elegant is the measure? Is it elegant in the <u>same way</u> other measures of symmetry within physics are elegant? Is this metric frame-invariant?
8. Does the measure imply how to measure anti-symmetry also- i.e., the mathematical property which corresponds to *negative* valence? (More on this in a bit)

Picking the *correct* symmetry measure that exactly corresponds to valence is currently outside the scope of this work. But we can list a few options:
- The most *a priori* elegant might be the size of the mathematical object's symmetry group, and I find this to be the most plausible approach. However, if mathematical objects which represent human phenomenologies tend to have large amounts of nodes, this measure would drop very quickly and would be implausible due to concern (2) above[22][23]. Possibly we could get around this by measuring symmetry piecemeal, per point (2.1).
- The simplest measure would be compressibility under standard compression algorithms (e.g., LZW/ZIP): all else being equal, more symmetric data structures will be more compressible.
- There exist many practical approximations for finding symmetry in graphs: e.g., Christoph Buchheim's notion of fuzzy symmetry detection, where he defines an algorithmic process for finding a 'closest symmetrical figure' and an 'edit distance' for how far the actual figure is from it. (Buchheim and Jünger 2004) This process would need to be adapted for the precise structure of Qualia space (a metric space?) but it seems to give the right *sort* of answer.
- Another option could be to use the idea of persistent homology (a statistical approach to understanding structure) to evaluate the *homogeneity* of the data in both 'local' and 'global' senses. (Carlsson 2009)

These just scratch the surface of possible approaches[24], and it may be too early in the exploration of Qualia space to settle on a single definition for symmetry/homogeneity. However, this may not turn out to be a particularly hard problem: all of these methods should give roughly similar results, symmetry detection is a very established and active area of research, and as IIT improves and gains more competitors I trust that our choice here will become easier. *In particular*, if we can solve the State Space Problem, this task may become trivial.

Is symmetry in our data structure really such a promising candidate for valence?
I expect most readers to find my symmetry hypothesis *prima facia* reasonable at this point. But for those who don't- for those who think symmetry is merely an intuition trap, i.e. something flashy-but-ultimately-shallow that might snare unwary theorists- I would say this:

Symmetry plays an absolutely central role in physics, on many levels. And so if consciousness is a physics problem, then we can say- *a priori*- that symmetry will play an absolutely central role in it, too, and seems likely to be matched with some qualia as important as valence. I'll defer to Max Tegmark and Frank Wilczek for a full-throated defense of this notion:

First, here's Wilczek describing overarching themes in physics:
Two obsessions are the hallmarks of Nature's artistic style:
- Symmetry--a love of harmony, balance, and proportion
- Economy--satisfaction in producing an abundance of effects from very limited means

---

[22] I still have some hope- see e.g., (Cohen, Dennett, and Kanwisher 2016) for discussion of how surprisingly sparse phenomenological experience may be. Also, the quicker phenomenological moments cycle through our consciousness, the smaller each could be. However, we couldn't use traditional tricks like edge pruning to boost the size of our symmetry group and still keep this measure elegant.
[23] If we can be confident this is the correct measure for pleasure, it would provide an invaluable tool for checking if a theory of consciousness is correct.
[24] A very easy-to-compute (although counter-intuitive) option was suggested by my friend Ryan Ragnar Thorngren, who noted we could use entropy as a rough proxy for symmetry. An excerpt: "Our first observation is that for probability distributions, the most symmetrical distribution is often the maximum entropy one. For example, the uniform distribution is both the unique translation-invariant measure and the maximum entropy distribution among all distributions." (Thorngren 2016) Similarly, Travis Dirks (personal discussion) has suggested that if we wish to measure the symmetry of a complex system, we should attempt to take advantage of something that's already happening- something the system is already computing. Perhaps for humans that would be qualia reports & revealed preferences.

Wilczek argues that symmetry in physical laws is not just a limited happenstance, but is woven throughout reality:
> … the idea that there *is* symmetry at the root of Nature has come to dominate our understanding of physical reality. We are led to a small number of special structures from purely mathematical considerations--considerations of symmetry--and put them forward to Nature, as candidate elements for her design.
>
> …
>
> In modern physics we have taken this lesson to heart. We have learned to work from symmetry toward truth. Instead of using experiments to infer equations, and then finding (to our delight and astonishment) that the equations have a lot of symmetry, we propose equations with enormous symmetry and then check to see whether Nature uses them. It has been an amazingly successful strategy. (Wilczek 2015)

Second, here's Max Tegmark (Chapter 12, Our Mathematical Universe) describing how much mileage physics has gotten out of studying symmetries in physical laws:
> "If we turn our attention to some particular mathematical structure [that describes a universe], how can we derive the physical properties that a self-aware observer in it would perceive it to have? In other words, how would an infinitely intelligent mathematician start with its mathematical definition and derive the physics description that we called the "consensus reality" in Chapter 9?
>
> We argued in Chapter 10 that her **first step would be to calculate what symmetries the mathematical structure has. Symmetry properties are among the very few types of properties that every mathematical structure possesses, and they can manifest themselves as physical symmetries to the structure's inhabitants.**
>
> The question of what she should calculate next when exploring an arbitrary structure is largely uncharted territory, but I find it striking that in the particular mathematical structure that we inhabit, further study of its symmetries has led to a gold mine of further insights. The German mathematician Emmy Noether proved in 1915 that **each continuous symmetry of our mathematical structure leads to a so-called conservation law of physics, whereby some quantity is guaranteed to stay constant**--and thereby have the sort of permanence that might make self-aware observers take note of it and give it a "baggage" name. All the conserved quantities that we discussed in Chapter 7 correspond to such symmetries: for example, energy corresponds to time-translation symmetry (that our laws of physics stay the same for all time), momentum corresponds to space-translation symmetry (that the laws are the same everywhere), angular momentum corresponds to rotation symmetry (that empty space has no special "up" direction) and electric charge corresponds to a certain symmetry of quantum mechanics. The Hungarian physicist Eugene Wigner went on to show that these symmetries also dictated all the quantum properties that particles can have, including mass and spin. In other words, between the two of them, Noether and Wigner showed that, at least in our own mathematical structure, studying the symmetries reveals what sort of "stuff" can exist in it. As I mentioned in Chapter 7, some physics colleagues of mine with a penchant for math jargon like to quip that a particle is simply "an element of an irreducible representation of the symmetry group." It's become clear that practically all our laws of physics originate in symmetries, and the physics Nobel laureate Philip Warren Anderson has gone even further, saying, **"It is only slightly overstating the case to say that physics is the study of symmetry."** [Emphases added.] (Tegmark 2014a)

These remarks by Wilczek and Tegmark don't prove (or even directly indicate) our hypothesis, but we could easily fill a book with quotes about how centrally important and unreasonably effective the study of symmetry is in physics, even if we limit our sources to Nobel Laureates. If consciousness research *is* a subset of physics- or even more generally, if consciousness research is merely *amenable to mathematical analysis*- symmetry is going to play a huge, possibly *dominant* role in it- period[25][26].

---

[25] Furthermore, if the symmetry of our mathematical-object-isomorphic-to-phenomenology *doesn't* correspond to valence, it should correspond to a quale *at least* as important (whatever that could be).

Symmetry vs asymmetry vs antisymmetry:
Mathematical objects can be *symmetric*, *asymmetric*, and *antisymmetric* in varying degrees, which I believe map to different positions in valence space. This corresponds to a triangle continuum:

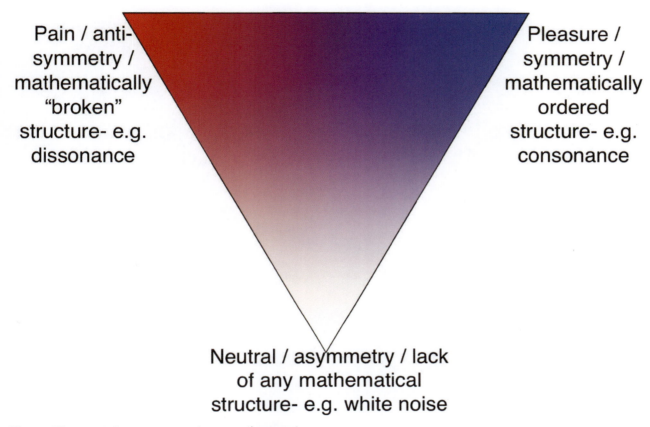

Figure 10: symmetry vs asymmetry vs antisymmetry.

We can explain this intuitively through an audio metaphor:
- We can think of symmetry as a major chord: full of elegant harmonic structure;
- We can think of antisymmetry as nails on a chalkboard: full of patterns which are actively dissonant with each other (frequencies that are "relatively prime" to each other);
- We can think of asymmetry as white noise: having no real structure which could exhibit consonance or dissonance.

For more on the mathematical structure of pleasing sound, and quantitative evidence that harmony is important, see (Tymoczko 2006); for an example technique for quantifying the consonance of arbitrary waveforms, see (Chon 2008).

So- if *symmetry/pleasure* is accurately approximated by one of the above metrics, could we also formalize and measure *antisymmetry/pain* and *asymmetry/neutral*, and combine these to fully specify a mind's location in valence space? In a word, yes. However, **_I worry that research into formalizing negative valence could be an information hazard_**, so I will leave it at this for now.

---

[26] As Weyl observed, "As far as I see, all a priori statements in physics have their origin in symmetry". (Weyl 1952)

A structural tradeoff between valence and degree of consciousness:

An interesting implication we get if we take our hypothesis and apply it to IIT is that if we attempt to *maximize* pleasure/symmetry, consciousness/Φ drops very rapidly. I.e., a fully symmetric system has no room for the sort of complexity necessary for integrated information. This is consistent with the phenomenological observation that pleasurable experiences / flow states involve time compression, and vice-versa.

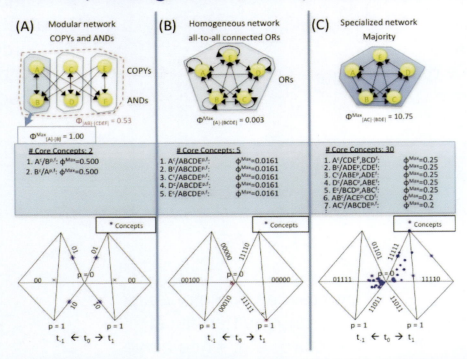

Figure 11: symmetry *vs* Φ, graphic from (Oizumi, Albantakis, and Tononi 2014). Note the high symmetry and low Φ of (A) and (B), vs the high Φ and low symmetry of (C).

This gives us some guidance on how to define the more general state-space of valence*intensity*consciousness:

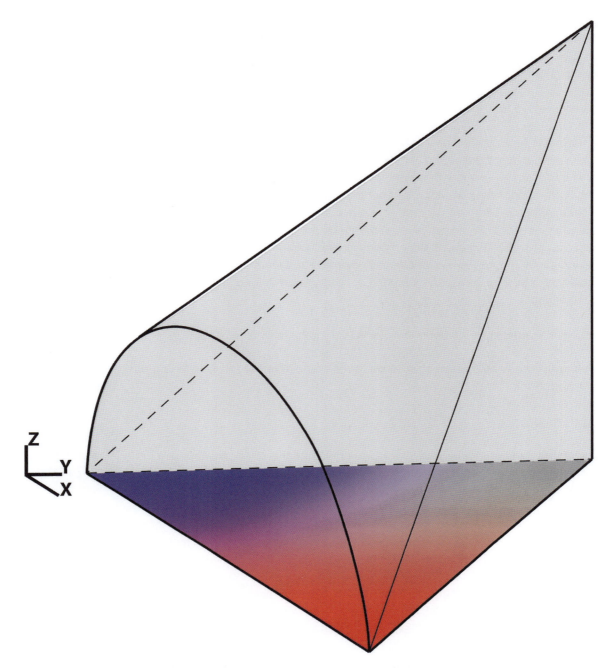

Figure 12, the state-space of valence*intensity*consciousness. X is the valence axis (the degree to which the structure is symmetric/ordered vs anti-symmetric/dissonant/disordered), Y is the intensity axis (the degree to which the symmetric vs anti-symmetric distinction applies at all), and Z is the degree-of-consciousness[27] axis (the amount of integrated information, if we assume the IIT framework).

What people generally refer to when they speak of 'happiness' or 'suffering' - the *morally significant hedonic status* of a system- is the *product* of valence*intensity*consciousness, or the location within this *combined* state-space.

---

[27] My friend Andres suggests that we could also conceptualize the consciousness axis as the degree to which a system's operation leaves records or has features that can be recalled (personal discussion). E.g., intense conscious-but-non-recallable experiences may exist.

XI. Testing this hypothesis today

In a perfect world, we could plug many peoples' real-world IIT-style datasets into a symmetry detection algorithm and see if this "Symmetry in the Topology of Phenomenology" (SiToP) theory of valence successfully predicted their self-reported valences.

Unfortunately, we're a long way from having the theory and data to do that.

But if we make two fairly modest assumptions, I think we should be able to perform some reasonable, simple, and elegant tests on this hypothesis *now*. The two assumptions are:
   (1) We can probably assume that symmetry/pleasure is a more-or-less *fractal* property: i.e., it'll be evident on basically *all* locations and scales of our data structure, and so it should be obvious even with imperfect measurements. Likewise, symmetry in one part of the brain will imply symmetry elsewhere, so we may only need to measure it in a small section that need not be directly contributing to consciousness.
   (2) We can probably assume that symmetry in connectome-level brain networks / activity will roughly imply symmetry in the mathematical-object-isomorphic-to-phenomenology (the symmetry that 'matters' for valence), and vice-versa. I.e., we need not worry too much about the exact 'flavor' of symmetry we're measuring.

So- given these assumptions, I see three ways to test our hypothesis:

1. More pleasurable brain states should be more compressible (all else being equal).
Ease of testing: 8/10
Safety: 10/10
Fidelity of data: 4/10

Symmetry implies compressibility, and so if we can measure the compressibility of a brain state in some sort of broad-stroke fashion while controlling for degree of consciousness, this should be a fairly good proxy for how pleasant that brain state is.

(Casali et al. 2013) defines a relevant metric called the "Perturbational Complexity Index" (PCI, or "zap and zip") which involves 'zapping' a brain with TMS, measuring the resulting activity via high-density EEG, then 'zipping' it-- seeing how well this EEG data compresses:

> "We determined the PCI in individual patients by performing several steps (Fig. 1): (i) recording the brain's early reaction (within the first 300 ms) to a direct TMS-induced cortical perturbation with high-density electroencephalography (hd-EEG) (25); (ii) performing source modeling and nonparametric statistics to extract a binary matrix of significant sources [SS(x,t)] that describes the spatiotemporal pattern of activation caused by the TMS perturbation (26); (iii) compressing this matrix to calculate its information content with algorithmic complexity measures, such as the Lempel-Ziv complexity index (27); and (iv) normalizing algorithmic complexity by the source entropy of SS(x,t) (28). Thus, operationally, PCI is defined as the normalized Lempel-Ziv complexity of the spatiotemporal pattern of cortical activation triggered by a direct TMS perturbation (see the Supplementary Materials for details of these steps)."

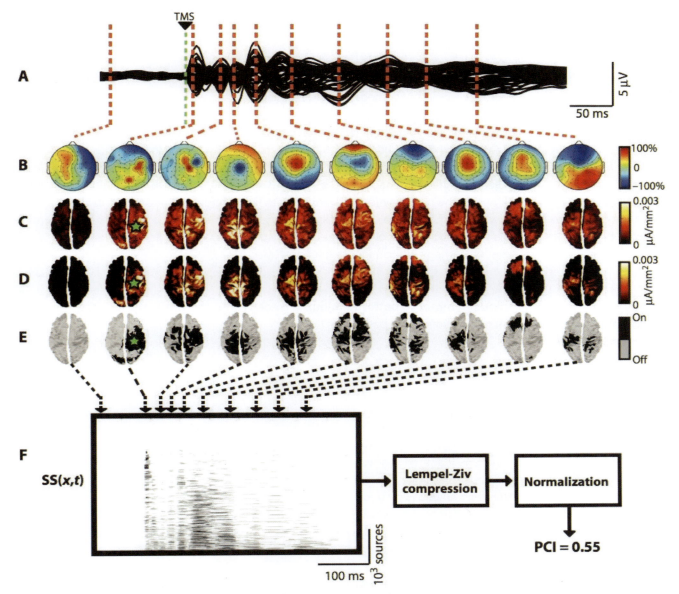

Fig. 1. The PCI is calculated from TMS-evoked potentials. (**A**) The black traces show the superposition of the averaged TMS-evoked potentials (150 trials) recorded from all EEG channels (butterfly plot of 60 channels) in one representative subject during wakefulness. (**B**) The color-coded maps show the instantaneous voltage distributions at selected latencies [auto-scaled between the maximum (+100%) and the minimum (−100%) instantaneous voltages]. (**C**) The corresponding distributions of cortical currents are calculated by means of a weighted minimum norm inverse solution applied to a three-sphere BERG forward model. (**D**) Significant TMS-evoked cortical currents are estimated by applying a nonparametric bootstrap-based statistical procedure at the source level. (**E**) A binary spatio-temporal distribution of significant sources (SS) is extracted: $SS(x,t) = 1$ for significant sources (x) and time samples (t); $SS(x,t) = 0$ otherwise. The sources in the matrix $SS(x,t)$ are sorted, from bottom to top, on the basis of their total activity during the post-stimulus period. (**F**) The information content of SS is estimated by calculating the Lempel-Ziv complexity measure (see fig. S3 for a diagram of the algorithm). PCI is defined as the information content of SS, normalized by the correspondent source entropy. Green star, site of TMS stimulation.

Figure 13: Casali et al.'s method for testing compressibility under TMS.

We define two general predictions with regard to compressibility:
(1) Under Casali's PCI method above, insofar as a given person's brain states are pleasant going into the TMS, the data from their hd-EEG will be more compressible (assuming that we control for the subjects' degree of consciousness*);
(2) If we skip the TMS step entirely, insofar as a given person's brain states are pleasant their hd-EEG data will be more compressible (assuming that we control for the subjects' degree of consciousness*).

*How do we "control for the subjects' degree of consciousness"? It's not clear that we can rely on self-reports, or external evaluations, for this. Probably the best way forward would be to find a reference task which involves a certain type of problem-solving which encourages a certain degree of consciousness- though I don't have a clear solution in mind yet. It's possible that trying to control for degree of consciousness might add more noise to the experiment than it would remove, so perhaps we can ignore it for now.

2. Highly consonant/harmonious/symmetric patterns injected directly into the brain should feel dramatically better than similar but dissonant patterns.
Ease of testing: 2/10
Safety: 5/10
Fidelity of data: 8/10

Consonance in audio signals generally produces positive valence; dissonance (e.g., nails-on-a-chalkboard) reliably produces negative valence. This obviously follows from our hypothesis, but it's also obviously true, so we can't use it as a novel prediction. But if we take the general idea and apply it to unusual ways of 'injecting' a signal into the brain, we should be able to make predictions that are (1) novel, and (2) practically useful.

TMS is generally used to *disrupt* brain functions by oscillating a strong magnetic field over a specific region to make those neurons fire chaotically. But if we used it on a lower-powered, rhythmic setting to 'inject' a symmetric/consonant pattern directly into parts of the brain involved directly with consciousness, the result should produce good feeling- or at least, much *better* valence than a similar dissonant pattern.

Our specific prediction: direct, low-power, rhythmic stimulation (via TMS) of the thalamus at harmonic frequencies (e.g., @1hz+2hz+4hz+6hz+8hz+12hz+16hz+24hz+36hz+48hz+72hz+96hz+148hz) should feel significantly more pleasant than similar stimulation at dissonant frequencies (e.g., @1.01hz+2.01hz+3.98hz+6.02hz+7.99hz+12.03hz+16.01hz+24.02hz+35.97hz+48.05hz+72.04hz+95.94hz+147.93hz).

Factors to keep in mind:
- The amount of pre-processing a stimulus undergoes before it hits a "consciousness center" matters a lot: we predict this is a big reason why auditory harmony more reliably produces pleasant valence than visual harmony/symmetry. I.e., visual data has a much longer pre-processing pipeline, with lots of feature-detectors which will munge the structure of the original stimulus.
- In addition to the length of the preprocessing pipeline, it's important to note that visual data has a base structure which is much more complex and multi-modal (~2.5d space + 3 color vectors + time) than audio, so it's more difficult to encode- and define- 'true' (i.e., multi-modal) symmetries in visual stimuli.
- It seems plausible that skipping *all* pre-processing by directly stimulating brain networks with a simple highly-symmetric pattern may produce an effect *much stronger* than auditory consonance.
- On the other hand, direct stimulation to consciousness centers such as the thalamus has been shown to disrupt consciousness very effectively, and this may be true even at very low intensities. It could be that we'll

be forced to stimulate a route or region that's merely *close* to the thalamus instead- e.g., the vagus nerve, or directly-neighboring region. Obviously direct stimulation of the 'pleasure centers' would likely produce pleasure, but the point is to test *patterns*, not *anatomy*.

- Direct harmonic stimulation of the auditory cortex would be instructive as well.
- Direct stimulation of certain frequencies is likely to trigger physiological mechanisms which regulate gamma waves, serotonin release, etc, and we need to control for this as best we can to isolate the symmetry-based effects. Contrasting the effects of stimulation with very similar waveforms- one tuned to be harmonic, the other to be dissonant- *should* control for most of this.
- We might not need to hit the pattern exactly-- perhaps we can just get it close to an attractor basin, and let the brain's natural dynamics do the rest.[28] If this is true, we might also need to turn the stimulation off quickly, or have some adaptive feedback after getting it close, to prevent dissonance between our signal and the specific symmetry the brain's attractor basin is optimizing for.
- The stronger the external stimulation, the less the specific network connectivity may matter. I.e., the effective causality of the system is being altered.[29] This could increase concerns about subjects being able to give true reports about their qualia.
- Stochastically altering the firing threshold of a consciousness center with a structured one-dimensional stimulation pattern is a very crude way to increase symmetry compared to what we could do with adaptive logic & electrode arrays, or with even more sophisticated technology. The above test intended as a relatively simple proof-of-concept.
- A positive result could lead to interesting new paths in musical development and pain management, among other things.

3. More consonant vagus nerve stimulation (VNS) should feel better than dissonant VNS.
Ease of testing: 9/10
Safety: 8/10
Fidelity of data: 3/10

The above harmonics-based TMS method would be a 'pure' test of the 'Symmetry in the Topology of Phenomenology' (SiToP) hypothesis. It may rely on developing custom hardware and is also well outside of my research budget.

However, a promising alternative method to test this is with consumer-grade vagus nerve stimulation (VNS) technology. Nervana Systems[30] has an in-ear device which stimulates the Vagus nerve with rhythmic electrical pulses as it winds its way past the left ear canal. The stimulation is synchronized with either user-supplied music or ambient sound. This synchronization is done, according to the company, in order to mask any discomfort associated with the electrical stimulation. The company says their system works by "electronically signal[ing] the Vagus nerve which in turn stimulates the release of neurotransmitters in the brain that enhance mood."

This explanation isn't very satisfying, since it merely punts the question of why these neurotransmitters enhance mood, but their approach seems to work-- and based on the symmetry/harmony hypothesis we can say at least something about *why*: effectively, they've somewhat accidentally built a synchronized bimodal approach (coordinated combination of music+VNS) for inducing harmony/symmetry in the brain. This is certainly not the only component of how this VNS system functions, since the parasympathetic nervous system is both complex and powerful by itself, but it could be an *important* component.

Based on our assumptions about what valence is, we can make a hierarchy of predictions:

---

[28] Thanks to Randal Koene and Stephen Frey for this insight.
[29] Thanks to Randal Koene for this interpretation.
[30] There are other options on the horizon as well- e.g., "V1bes, inc" has a TMS-based VNS device in beta.

1. Harmonious music + synchronized VNS should feel the best;
2. Harmonious music + placebo VNS (unsynchronized, simple pattern of stimulation) should feel less pleasant than (1);
3. Harmonious music + non-synchronized VNS (stimulation that is synchronized to a *different* kind of music) should feel less pleasant than (1);
4. Harmonious music + dissonant VNS (stimulation with a pattern which scores low on consonance measures such as (Chon 2008) should feel worse than (2) and (3);
5. Dissonant auditory noise + non-synchronized, dissonant VNS should feel pretty awful.

We can also predict that if a bimodal approach for inducing harmony/symmetry in the brain is better than a single modality, a trimodal or quadrimodal approach may be even more effective. E.g., we should consider testing the addition of synchronized rhythmic tactile stimulation and symmetry-centric music visualizations. A key question here is whether adding stimulation modalities would lead to diminishing or synergistic/accelerating returns.

Part III - Discussion

XII. Taking stock

So far, this work has reviewed what we know about valence & consciousness, synthesized a novel modular framework for understanding consciousness research, and offered a hypothesis about valence based on this framework.

What's happening now in qualia research:
Within academia, there are three primary active lines of approach in quantitative qualia research:
- Tononi is continuing to pitch IIT's relevance for explaining NCC data, and is also working on improving how IIT handles 'relations', or what happens when systems overlap;
- Tsuchiya's lab is working on developing more-easily-computable approximations for integrated information, especially those which can be applied to neural data (Haun et al. 2016; Oizumi et al. 2016). They've suggested that category theory may be somehow useful to understand the nature of the output (Tsuchiya, Taguchi, and Saigo 2016)- though with no specific predictions yet- and will be doing larger-scale simulations in the future.
- Tegmark is also working on more-easily-computable approximations for integrated information (Tegmark 2016) and on his Perceptronium approach to reconstructing integrated information from interactions in quantum physics (Tegmark 2015). Others are exploring other possibilities for turning IIT into a more physical theory, for example (A. B. Barrett 2014) argues for reframing IIT as a quantum field theory, specifically that consciousness arises from integrated information in the electromagnetic field.[31]

These lines of research are promising, but also narrow, and I think there are substantial benefits to taking a "full-stack" approach as I've done in this work. The pilot project for this full-stack approach is the mystery of valence, and the output of this is the Symmetry in the Topology of Phenomenology (SiToP) hypothesis- or more simply, the Symmetry Hypothesis of Valence.

Evaluating my hypothesis on valence:
SiToP is a description of valence which will be counter-intuitive to many, built atop a framework for consciousness which is counter-intuitive to many. Obviously, I don't think intuition should be the primary evaluation criteria. But how *should* we evaluate it? I propose the following:
- We should consider the principles & their inverses:
    - Are the principles reasonable?
    - What would knowledge about qualia & valence look like if each of the principles *wasn't* true?
- We should consider common alternative frameworks:
    - Do they assume the problem I define is soluble? If so, what would knowledge about qualia look like under each alternative?
    - How good is each alternative? And do they actually make predictions or engage in motte-and-bailey style moves?
- We should evaluate if it describes a consistent worldview:
    - Is it internally consistent?
    - Is it consistent with ontologies it *will* eventually need to be consistent with (e.g., physics)?
- We should consider if it extends scientific knowledge to new contexts in a similar way to how science has been extended before;

---

[31] Exploring the physics of consciousness is an ongoing interest of our research collective in California, and I would point toward the good work done by Andres Gomez Emilsson.

- And most importantly, we should consider the predictions it makes, explicitly and implicitly:
    - I.e., does it actually *make* clear predictions?
    - … and are they *correct*?
    - Is it extensible enough to eventually either answer or dissolve any arbitrary question about qualia?
    - Are there any easy ways to test this hypothesis that I've missed?

I'm confident my framework, heuristics, and hypothesis do much better on the above criteria than any other current option. But this may simply reflect the state of the field.

How my hypothesis may help generate new hypotheses about neuroanatomy and neurochemistry:

A full reinterpretation of how neuroanatomy and neurochemistry combine to generate pain and pleasure in light of my hypothesis is beyond the scope of this work. However, I would suggest the following very general themes:

On the anatomy & network topology of valence:
My hypothesis strongly implies that 'hedonic' brain regions influence mood by virtue of acting as 'tuning knobs' for symmetry/harmony in the brain's consciousness centers. Likewise, nociceptors, and the brain regions which gate & interpret their signals, will be located at critical points in brain networks, able to cause large amounts of salience-inducing antisymmetry very efficiently. We should also expect rhythm to be a powerful tool for modeling brain dynamics involving valence- for instance, we should be able to extend (Safron 2016)'s model of rhythmic entrainment in orgasm to other sorts of pleasure.[32]

More speculatively…

On valence & neuropharmacology:
Non-opioid painkillers and anti-depressants are complex, but it may turn out that a core mechanism by which they act is by introducing noise into neural activity and connectivity, respectively. This would explain the odd findings that acetaminophen blunts acute pleasure (Durso, Luttrell, and Way 2015), and that anti-depressants can induce long-term affective flattening[33].

This would also predict that psychedelic substances, although often pleasurable, actually increase emotional *variance* by biasing the brain toward symmetrical structure, and could result in enhanced *pain* if this structure is then broken-- i.e., they are in this sense the *opposite* of painkillers. Additionally, we *may* find that some uncomfortable sensations are caused by 'competing symmetries'- patterns that are internally symmetrical but not symmetrical to each other, which would predict complex and sometimes destructive interactions between different normally-pleasurable activities and psychoactives.

Furthermore, I would anticipate that severe tinnitus could lead to affective flattening for similar interference-based reasons: insofar as the brain's subconscious preprocessing can't tune it out, the presence of a constant pattern in consciousness would likely make it more difficult to generate symmetries (valence) on-the-fly. This would also imply that the specific frequency pattern of the perceived tinnitus sensation may matter more than is commonly assumed.

On self-organization & deep learning:

---

[32] My expectation is that people with musical anhedonia (~2-5% of the population) may have an abnormal auditory preprocessing pipeline that significantly alters the structure of auditory stimuli before it gets to a consciousness center. I.e., music effectively 'hacks' valence partly because it's highly patterned (symmetrical), and people who have musical anhedonia will have a non-standard ear-to-thalamus pipeline that breaks these sorts of patterns.

[33] My friend Andres Gomez Emilsson suggests this could be due to upregulation of agmatine (personal discussion).

My hypothesis implies that symmetry/harmony is a core component of the brain's organizational & computational syntax: specifically, we should think of symmetry as one (of many) dynamic attractors in the brain.[34]

This suggests that mammals got a bit lucky that we evolved to seek out pleasure! But not *that* lucky, since symmetry is a very *functionally-relevant and useful* property for systems to self-organize around, for at least two reasons:

First, self-organizing systems such as the brain must develop some way to perform error-correction, measure & maintain homeostasis, and guide & constrain morphological development. Symmetry-as-a-dynamic-attractor is a profoundly powerful solution to all of these which could evolve in incrementally-useful forms, and so symmetry-seeking seems like a common, perhaps nigh-universal evolutionary path to take[35]. Indeed, it might be exceedingly difficult to develop a system with complex adaptive traits *without* heavy reliance upon principles of symmetry.[36]

Second, the brain embodies principles of symmetry because it's an efficient structure for modeling our world. (Lin and Tegmark 2016) note that physics and deep learning neural networks display cross-domain parallels such as "symmetry, locality, compositionality and polynomial log-probability", and that deep learning can often avoid combinatorial explosion due to the fact that the physical world has lots of predictable symmetries, which enable unusually efficient neural network encoding schemes.

On Boredom:
Why do we find pure order & symmetry boring, and *not* particularly beautiful? I posit *boredom is a very sophisticated "anti-wireheading" technology* which prevents the symmetry/pleasure attractor basin from being too 'sticky', and may be activated by an especially low rate of Reward Prediction Errors (RPEs). Musical features which add mathematical variations or imperfections to the structure of music-- e.g., syncopated rhythms (Witek et al. 2014), vocal burrs, etc-- seem to make music more addictive and allows us to find long-term pleasure in listening to it, by hacking the mechanic(s) by which the brain implements boredom.

These notions paint with a broad brush, and it's important to reiterate the caveats mentioned in Section XI- that the symmetry that 'matters' for pleasure is the symmetry in the mathematical object isomorphic to phenomenology, not in neural circuits themselves, and that only the networks/substrates that are actively contributing to consciousness (e.g., IIT's MIP) directly 'count' towards qualia and valence.

Other notable research directions: ethics and AI safety

If we define ethics as the study of what is intrinsically valuable, it would be a notable understatement to say that understanding consciousness & valence seem critically important for having a non-insane theory of ethics. The task of understanding the good- and treating sentient creatures better- both seem to require understanding valence (see e.g., (Johnson 2015a)).

---

[34] By implication, humans are not *strictly speaking* pleasure-maximizers… but we do *tend to* work to increase our valence, satisficing against our other dynamic attractors.
[35] This is not to say evolution uses or generates symmetry in straightforward ways: the details of how symmetry is realized in biological networks may involve complex methods by which stochastic & asymmetric processes on one level generate symmetry on another: see, e.g., (Nishikawa and Motter 2016).
[36] As a very 'primitive' part of the brain, we can predict that the limbic system is likely built up from simple, more implicit, easy-to-coordinate heuristics such as symmetry (compared to the neocortex, where layered hierarchical control has had the opportunity to evolve). Indeed, this may help explain why the limbic system is so associated with emotion- we can expect that (1) symmetry is a relatively large part of the mechanism by which it performs control and interoception, and (2) symmetries form more easy there (compared to e.g., the neocortex)..

Another particularly pressing problem in ethics is AI safety's 'Value Problem', or the question of what normative values we should instill into future artificial intelligences in order to make them friendly to humans. Currently, the state of the art here is indirect normativity, or building systems to teach artificial intelligences what humans value based on watching how humans behave & interact. Unfortunately, this is prone to problems common to machine learning paradigms (e.g., overfitting, proper model selection, etc) as well as the problem of human values being inherently fuzzy and internally inconsistent.

For humans, the fact that our values are fuzzy & internally inconsistent is troublesome- but if we build future artificial intelligences that are substantially smarter & more capable than we are, instilling the wrong values in them could easily lead to futures that include neither humans nor anything intrinsically valuable.

Max Tegmark has noted that since we're made out of physical 'stuff', the Value Problem is ultimately a physics problem. He suggests reframing this question as 'what makes certain arrangements of particles better than other arrangements?' However, he notes that we don't yet have a clue how to approach this "simpler" question either, and this is an existential threat:

> In summary, we have yet to identify any final goal for our Universe that appears both definable and desirable. The only currently programmable goals that are guaranteed to remain truly well-defined as the AI gets progressively more intelligent are goals expressed in terms of physical quantities alone: particle arrangements, energy, entropy, causal entropy, etc. However, we currently have no reason to believe that any such definable goals will be desirable by guaranteeing the survival of humanity. *Contrariwise, it appears that we humans are a historical accident, and aren't the optimal solution to any well-defined physics problem. This suggests that a superintelligent AI with a rigorously defined goal will be able to improve its goal attainment by eliminating us.* This means that to wisely decide what to do about AI-development, we humans need to confront not only traditional computational challenges, but also some of the most obdurate questions in philosophy. To program a self-driving car, we need to solve the trolley problem of whom to hit during an accident. To program a friendly AI, we need to capture the meaning of life. What is "meaning"? What is "life"? What is the ultimate ethical imperative, i.e., how should we strive to shape the future of our Universe? If we cede control to a superintelligence before answering these questions rigorously, the answer it comes up with is unlikely to involve us. (Tegmark 2014b)

Research on consciousness & valence by itself won't *solve* issues of ethics, AI safety, personal identity, meaning, social health, and how to use the atoms in our light-cone, but this research does seem *centrally necessary* for *good* answers to these questions, and provides a way to cut through confusion and build useful tools. I sketch out some initial thoughts on how valence research can help AI safety in (Johnson 2015b).[37]

And if the arguments about consciousness and valence in this work are substantially correct, we should be approaching both ethics and AI safety research very differently than we are now.

XIII. Closing thoughts

There are an enormous number of further technical clarifications, potential extensions, items currently lacking in the IIT ecosystem, and strategic implications we could explore- and I and some friends plan to, in subsequent works. But

---

[37] Looking further ahead, if we can ground ethics in consciousness research, merge consciousness research with physics, and codify ethically-relevant properties of physical systems in machine-readable forms, it'll open up a lot of options for designing safer AIs and more ethical societies. Examples range from AI utility functions that penalize the creation of strongly low-valence states, to valence-aware smart contracts, to valence-positive cryptocurrency mining (thanks to Karl Hiner for this latter idea).

for now, I want to close with some brief thoughts about a new 'Science of Qualia'.

In short, all common ways science talks about consciousness are manifestly insane. We speak as if high-level functions and sensations are neatly localized in anatomy; we speak as if neurotransmitters like Serotonin and Dopamine have clean effect profiles; we speak as if finding neural correlates of consciousness (NCC) is a 'real' sort of knowledge that we can build a science around. These things are true only in a very lossy, noisy sense- and are a terrible basis for formalizing a science of qualia.

In this work and its appendices, I've sketched out what I think a "non-insane" Science of Qualia should look like- something that could turn qualia research from alchemy into chemistry, and unify our different modes of knowing in neuroscience.

We just have to follow-through and build it.

Appendix A: Remarks on the Vocabulary Problem
"What are some guiding principles for how to improve our language about phenomenology so as to 'carve reality at the joints'?"

A big problem facing qualia research is that the words we use now to describe our experience/qualia won't tend to "carve reality at the joints", so we may have to create a new vocabulary bit by bit as we learn more about what sorts of qualia are "natural kinds".

I.e., we may find a crisp geometric distinction in our data structure which should correspond to something interesting in the qualia domain, and it might *in fact* have a corresponding quale, but it'll be likely we won't already have a crisp word for this quale. Much of future qualia research may involve *coining, amalgamating,* or *differentiating* terms in order to bring our phenomenological vocabularies closer to correspondence with the actual structure of reality.

Toward a 'Periodic Table of Qualia'
A plausible analogy for how we currently talk about qualia is how the ancients talked of chemistry before the Periodic Table. Before we had a grasp on the underlying chemistry at work, we sometimes had lots of different words for the same underlying thing (e.g., the ancients spoke about different forms of carbon, like charcoal, graphite, and diamond, as if they were fundamentally different), one word for fundamentally different things (e.g., the ancients commonly conflated Bismuth, Antimony, Tin, and Lead)- and no word at all for still other things (e.g., we're surrounded by Argon in the atmosphere, but it wasn't 'discovered' until 1895). Going further back in time, we thought of certain things (Air+Earth+Fire+Water, and the five Platonic Solids) as the atomic basis for reality, and in retrospect we were quite confused. If we want to get a feel for how we'll speak about phenomenology in the future, we can possibly extrapolate based on the ways our chemical vocabulary evolved as we figured things out.

The key insight which allowed us to turn alchemy into chemistry was the discovery of patterns in reactivity, which ended up being due to electron shell configuration, and this observation formed the basis for the Periodic Table and speaking about chemical substances in a crisp way.

My hypothesis is that an analogous organizing principle for qualia, which will allow our words to better 'carve reality at the joints', is that we should think of qualia in geometric & topological ways- i.e., our future vocabulary for phenomenology will borrow heavily from 'terms of art' in branches of math such as geometry and topology, just as physics did in the 20th century.

Appendix B: Remarks on the Translation Problem
"Given a mathematical object isomorphic to a system's phenomenology, how do we populate a translation list between its mathematical properties and the part of phenomenology each property or pattern corresponds to?"

Or more succinctly, *how do we connect the quantitative with the qualitative?*

In Section VIII I sketched out a heuristic for making distinctions in the qualia domain by enumerating topological properties, and made the following suggestions: qualia may be *simple* vs *complex*, *atomic* vs *composite*, and *local* vs *global, intuitively important* vs *intuitively trivial*, and these distinctions will apply equally to both qualia and their corresponding geometric representation.

The picture this implies is that knowledge about qualia will (at least initially[38]) take the form of a translation table between geometric/topological properties, and their corresponding phenomena in the qualia domain.

---

[38] This 'translation table' approach is crude and lossy, and is to be supplanted by something more elegant ASAP.

Here are a few *very speculative* possible starting points, of unknown quality:[39]

Assorted <u>mathematical properties</u> of the quantitative representation of a conscious system's phenomenology (e.g., IIT's output):	<u>Qualia</u> these properties correspond to:
Height/magnitude	Degree of consciousness (per Tononi)
Symmetry(global)[40]	Positive valence (per Section X of this paper)
Anti-symmetry(global)	Negative valence?
Symmetry(local)	?
Curvature(global,local)	?
Ratio[effective dimensionality:maximum dimensionality](global,local)	?
Entropy increasing vs decreasing	?
?	Surprise
Complex (chaotic) coalition-based dynamic system with well-defined attractors and a high level of criticality (low activation energy needed to switch between attractors)* + internal model of self-as-agent + can't predict itself	Free Will[41]
Particular geometric arrangements- e.g., Mark's idea of "fan in" vs "fan out"	?
?	Love/empathy/connectedness
Geometric texture metrics(global,local), phase transitions & integration between features of object	Certain psychological "glosses"- e.g., 3d space, separation of objects, perceptions of duration and change, normal vs non-dual[42] consciousness?
Representational properties(local)	Being 'aware' of certain objects/sensations
Semi-local properties?	Redness, sweetness, etc

This above list is a bare handful of speculative mappings, described at a high and lossy level of abstraction. How do we improve it, and populate this list in a richer, more systematic, and more precise way? A comprehensive explanation of how to do so is outside the scope of this work, but we can say a few things in the meantime.

---

[39] Thanks to Randal Koene for pushing me to generalize other hypotheses in addition to valence.
[40] By implication, Valence Formalism is true insofar as there always exists a preferred measure of symmetry.
[41] It seems plausible that most systems with high criticality would have a *relatively* high amount of integrated information- so most systems experiencing the dynamics of Free Will would get some amount of consciousness 'for free'. The reverse may also be true.
[42] An important component of how meditation produces positive valence may be that it simplifies and shrinks the phenomenological sense of self, which is one fewer thing external patterns can produce dissonance with.

The simplest method is to simply do *more* of what we were doing in Sections VIII and IX, but further expanding our list of distinctions, and looking for properties *other* than valence.[43] Over time, we can build up a list of geometric/topological properties and the phenomenology they may map to (following Chalmers, we can call each of these pairs a *psychophysical law*).

Importantly, this allows us to either start from geometry/topology and trying to figure out corresponding phenomenology, or start from phenomenology and trying to figure out corresponding geometry/topology. Progress here is highly dependent upon addressing the Vocabulary Problem. Some threads we may pull here:
1. Studying techniques, distinctions, and terms of art in topology and geometry (e.g., curvature, homotopy, etc) may help generate further distinctions which map to the qualia domain;
2. Any progress we can make on the State Space Problem will give us more knowledge of the structure of qualia (see Appendix D);
3. Evaluating the geometry & topology of our senses (e.g., (Gomez Emilsson 2015a) may help us form hypotheses about how they are embedded into the mathematical object representing our phenomenology;
4. We should aim to connect this 'translation table' approach with the existing body of NCC literature, to produce rules of thumb for which sorts of network topologies generate which sorts of qualia (see (Bullmore and Sporns 2009) for a discussion of graph topologies in brain networks) and to build dynamical models of qualia;
5. We can evaluate various sorts of psychological 'glosses' and trying to work backwards to the sorts of geometric textures, phase transitions, and integration between features of the mathematical object they may correspond with- e.g., see (Gomez Emilsson 2016) for a hypothesis about how psychedelics perturb psychological glosses and how this may help reveal underlying structure. Similarly, Anil K. Seth's work on predictive coding and top-down vs bottom-up processes, and our layered models of the self, might be able to inspire mathematical hypotheses about global vs local properties of qualia;
6. We could data-mine phenomenological reports (e.g., psychedelic experiences, psychological experiments and therapy reports, romance novels, philosophers like Husserl, etc) for terms that have geometric connotations and try to match these terms with the qualia people seemed to be experiencing at that time;
7. If we're *certain* of an exact translation pair- e.g., if we *know* that valence is a specific formulation of symmetry- we could use this known data-point to check whether IIT is doing the math right;
8. A rising strategy in neuroscience is (with a nod to Michael Graziano) to approach qualia from the perspective of "what kind of system would generate this kind of self-description?" - we should attempt to merge this attention-schema heuristic with whatever formal models of ground-truth qualia we can muster.

Most of these strategies are rather imperfect, lossy, and noisy, and will be durably valuable only insofar as they allow us to make progress on *formalizing* qualia research. A good formalism itself can be surprisingly generative- here's Paul Dirac advocating a focus on formalization in physics research:
> The most powerful method of advance that can be suggested at present is to employ all the resources of pure mathematics in attempts to perfect and generalize the mathematical formalism that forms the existing basis of theoretical physics, and after each success in this direction, to try to interpret the new mathematical features in terms of physical entities. (Dirac 1931)

Appendix C: Remarks on the Reality Mapping Problem
"how do we choose a formal ontology for consciousness which can map unambiguously to reality?"

---

[43] If valence is the *c. elegans* of qualia, what is the *drosophila* of qualia? I.e., what's the next-easiest thing to reverse-engineer? (Thanks to Dan Barcay for this analogy.)

TL;DR version: Physics defines a privileged level of abstraction more 'real' than others, and is the proper ontology by which to define observer-moments. Incompatible levels of abstraction, such as computationalism & functionalism, which don't ultimately resolve to terms in physics, cannot support observer-moments.

The fundamental question in consciousness research is where to start. There are three ontologies which seem particularly relevant here: phenomenology (because that's what consciousness *is*), computation (since it seems like this is what consciousness *does*), and physics (because that's what the universe seem to be *made of*).

Phenomenology is helpful, but isn't a solution: there's a long tradition of addressing consciousness through phenomenology, spanning Buddhism, Berkeley, Hegel, and Whitehead. This tradition has only modest success: it's identified the *problem* of consciousness, and cleared up some forms of confusion about it, yet after thousands of years of trying, we *still* don't have a good formal ontology for talking about phenomenology. At best, phenomenology seems like a good source for *inspiration* and *validation* of theories of consciousness: e.g., Tononi notes that phenomenological observations were the inspiration for IIT's axioms.

Computationalism and physicalism are not the same:
The computing metaphor is absolutely dominant in today's society, and we tend to think of everything (including the brain) as a type of computer. This is often a very *useful* stance to take, but we should take great care in understanding what metaphysical assumptions this metaphor commits us to, and what our other options are. In particular, we should be crystal-clear that computationalism and physicalism lead in deeply incompatible directions and we should take great care in understanding the difference.[44]

Definitions:
Computationalism can be summarized as 'consciousness is what an algorithm feels like from the inside', and that we should understand consciousness in terms of *computation*. Importantly, algorithms can be run on multiple substrates, so this means that *any Turing-complete level of abstraction can generate consciousness*, given the right inputs.

Physicalism, on the other hand, argues that 'consciousness is what certain physical processes feel like from the inside', and that we should understand consciousness in terms of physics- e.g., quarks or strings. Importantly, this means consciousness is a *physical* phenomenon, just like electromagnetism or gravity, and there exists a privileged level of abstraction (physics) which is 'real' in a way that others (e.g., the outputs of high-level abstractions such as Turing machines) aren't.[45]

Physicalism's advantages: compatibility with physics (obviously) and frame-invariance.
For the purposes of my my hypothesis about valence, I'm agnostic between these choices insofar as they're each consistent with my assumptions in Section VII. But to put my cards on the table, I *am* a physicalist, and believe the only reasonable place to dig in and actually *formalize* an ontology for consciousness is physics, because computationalism is neither *frame-invariant* nor *commensurable with physics*, and thus fails the Reality Mapping Problem.

What is frame invariance?

---

[44] In particular, we should be careful not to say things such as 'consciousness is what the brain computes' or 'physics is just information being computed, thus if we talk about computation we're also talking about physics'. From a physicalist point of view, these are type errors that will invariably lead to confusion about the nature of consciousness.

[45] If physicalism is true, 'Turing complete' doesn't have anything to do with qualia. But if conscious systems (and their corresponding experiences) are limited by some constraint- e.g., the speed of light- then we could say interesting things about the finite set of qualia (personal discussion with Radhika Dirks), and also about how systems that were *'qualia complete'* could exist (e.g., Nozick's "experience machine").

A theory is frame-invariant if it doesn't depend on any specific physical frame of reference, or subjective interpretations to be true. Modern physics is frame-invariant in this way: the Earth's mass objectively exerts gravitational attraction on us regardless of how we choose to interpret it. Something like economic theory, on the other hand, is not frame-invariant: we must interpret how to apply terms such as "GDP" or "international aid" to reality, and there's always an element of subjective judgement in this interpretation, upon which observers can disagree.

<u>Why is frame invariance important in theories of mind?</u> *Because consciousness seems frame-invariant.* Your being conscious doesn't depend on my beliefs about consciousness, physical frame of reference, or interpretation of the situation-- if you are conscious, you are conscious *regardless* of these things. If I do something that hurts you, it hurts you *regardless* of my belief of whether I'm causing pain. Likewise, an octopus either is highly conscious, or isn't, regardless of my beliefs about it.[46] This implies that any ontology that has a chance of accurately describing consciousness must be frame-invariant, similar to how the formalisms of modern physics are frame-invariant.

In contrast, the way we map computations to physical systems seems inherently frame-dependent. To take a rather extreme example, if I shake a bag of popcorn, perhaps the motion of the popcorn's molecules could- under a certain interpretation- be mapped to computations which parallel those of a whole-brain emulation that's feeling pain. So am I computing anything by shaking that bag of popcorn? Who knows. Am I creating pain by shaking that bag of popcorn? Doubtful... but since there seems to be an unavoidable element of subjective judgment as to what constitutes information, and what constitutes computation, in actual physical systems, it doesn't seem like computationalism can *rule out* this possibility. Given this, computationalism is *frame-dependent* in the sense that there doesn't seem to be any objective fact of the matter derivable for what any given system is computing, even *in principle*.

What is ontological compatibility / commensurability?

Ontologies are compatible if one can be mapped/projected onto the other: for example, we can speak of biochemical processes in terms of quantum physics, or we can cleanly translate from a Mercator projection of Earth to a Cassini projection of Earth. Thomas Kuhn frames this in terms of *commensurability,* and argues that strictly speaking, most paradigms (ontologies) are *incommensurable* to each other because they use different taxonomic structures (they 'carve reality at different joints'). Examples of incommensurable ontologies which *don't* map cleanly to each other would be economics vs psychology, Linnaean vs genomic trees of life, and Aristotelian vs Newtonian definitions of motion.

<u>Why is incommensurability important in theories of mind?</u> If we try to explain consciousness in terms which are incommensurable with those of physics- i.e., if no clean mapping between our vocabulary and physical terms can be found- we'll never be able to apply our theories cleanly & unambiguously to *actual physical systems*. We'll never be able to precisely point to terms in our theory, and then point to corresponding stuff in a physical system, and say *this how my theory cashes out in actual reality.*[47] This is a big problem, and one that many theories of mind run into.

More generally, anytime we have two different ontologies and there's no crisp sort of mapping (e.g., an injection, surjection, bijection) between them, we will unavoidably run into what W.V.O. Quine calls the "indeterminacy of translation" (Van Orman Quine 1964), where we'll *necessarily* and *always* have multiple possible ways to interpret one ontology in terms of the other, and no principled way to choose between them.[48]

---

[46] However, we should be a little bit careful with the notion of 'objective existence' here if we wish to broaden our statement to include quantum-scale phenomena where choice of observer matters.
[47] Mitchell Porter on LessWrong.com suggests this is a form of dualism.
[48] Are frame-invariance and commensurability to physics coupled properties? I.e., if a theory is not frame-invariant, does this imply it's incommensurable with physics, and if a theory is frame-invariant in how it applies to reality, will it necessarily be commensurable with physics? This seems plausible.

IIT is neither frame-invariant nor commensurate with physics:
IIT is an odd hybrid which sits near the half-way mark between physicalism and computationalism: computationalists hold their nose at it since they see it as *too physicalist* & *realist* about consciousness, whereas physicalists also hold their nose as they see it as *too computationalist*. However, it is a Schelling Point for discussion as the most mature theory of consciousness we have, and I believe it suffers from the same core flaws as any computational theory of consciousness would, so we use its example to critique computationalism by proxy. Here's Max Tegmark (Tegmark 2015) on IIT's lack of frame-invariance:

> Despite its successes, Tononi's Integrated Information Theory (IIT) leaves many questions unanswered. If it is to extend our consciousness-detection ability to animals, computers and arbitrary physical systems, then we need to ground its principles in fundamental physics. IIT takes information, measured in bits, as a starting point. But when we view a brain or computer through our physicists eyes, as myriad moving particles, then what physical properties of the system should be interpreted as logical bits of information? I interpret as a "bit" both the position of certain electrons in my computer's RAM memory (determining whether the micro-capacitor is charged) and the position of certain sodium ions in your brain (determining whether a neuron is firing), but on the basis of what principle? Surely there should be some way of identifying consciousness from the particle motions alone, or from the quantum state evolution, even without this information interpretation? If so, what aspects of the behavior of particles corresponds to conscious integrated information?

Similarly, here's Adam Barrett (A. B. Barrett 2014) on ambiguities in IIT's application, and how IIT doesn't define information in a frame-invariant way:

> IIT has garnered substantial attention amongst consciousness researchers. However, it has been criticized for its proposed measures of integrated information not successfully being based on an intrinsic perspective (Gamez, 2011; Beaton and Aleksander, 2012; Searle, 2013). The proposed 'Φ' measures are applicable only to networks of discrete nodes, and thus for a complex system depend on the observer choosing a particular graining. More broadly, information can only be intrinsic to fundamental physical entities, and descriptions of information in systems modeled at a non-fundamental level necessarily rely on an extrinsic observer's choice of level (Floridi, 2009, 2010; Gamez, 2011).

Finally, in the process of critiquing Bostrom's Simulation Argument, Gordon McCabe (McCabe 2005) provides a general argument that defining physical processes in computational terms is an intractable problem. First, McCabe notes that:

> [T]here is a one-[to-]many correspondence between the logical states [of a computer] and the exact electronic states of computer memory. Although there are bijective mappings between numbers and the logical states of computer memory, there are no bijective mappings between numbers and the exact electronic states of memory.

This lack of bijective mapping means that subjective interpretation necessarily creeps in, and so a computational simulation of a physical system can't be 'about' that system in any *rigorous* way:

> In a computer simulation, the values of the physical quantities possessed by the simulated system are represented by the combined states of multiple bits in computer memory. However, the combined states of multiple bits in computer memory only represent numbers because they are deemed to do so under a numeric interpretation. There are many different interpretations of the combined states of multiple bits in computer memory. If the numbers represented by a digital computer are interpretation-dependent, they cannot be objective physical properties. Hence, there can be no objective relationship between the changing pattern of multiple bit-states in computer memory, and the changing pattern of quantity-values of a simulated physical system.

McCabe concludes that, metaphysically speaking,

> A digital computer simulation of a physical system cannot exist as, (does not possess the properties and relationships of), anything else other than a physical process occurring upon the components of a computer. In the contemporary case of an electronic digital computer, a simulation cannot exist as anything else other

than an electronic physical process occurring upon the components and circuitry of a computer. (McCabe 2005)

The bottom line:
Since there will *always* be multiple valid interpretations of how IIT 3.0 & computationalism applies to a given physical system, they can never be unambiguously applied to actual physical systems even *in principle*. I take this as a *reductio ad absurdum* and believe we should treat them merely as inspirational stand-ins for more correct *physical* theories of mind.

I would love to be proven wrong, however, and would challenge Tononi et al. to give an example of precisely how IIT would apply to a toy quantum system, in a way that follows naturally from the axioms.[49] Likewise, I would challenge computationalists to look into principled ways of answering the following questions:
- How can we enumerate which computations are occurring in a given physical system?
    - How can we establish that a given computation is *not* occurring in a physical system?
        - If some computations 'count' toward qualia and others don't, what makes them 'count'?
- How can we match which computations are generating which qualia?
- What is a frame-invariant (non-subjective) way to determine system equivalence for qualia?

… thus stands our argument against computationalism. But we still need to address the core reason why people are driven *away from physicalism*: the problem of epiphenomenalism and qualia reports.

The curious case of qualia reports, downward causation, & computationalism
A popular argument for computationalism is that, since we can report our qualia, they must have causal power. Proponents argue that this *ability to report about our qualia* is a fundamental fact any theory of consciousness must address, and that there's a natural synergy with computationalism with how computational threads can recursively monitor themselves.

Straightforward *physical* theories of qualia, on the other hand, don't have any such 'strongly emergent recursion' built in, and instead seem to identify qualia as merely *epiphenomenal*. Epiphenomenalism is generally used as an epithet in this context, and refers to how if physics gives rise to qualia, then in a significant sense all qualia is 'just along for the ride' and can't affect the physical world. This seems false to us, since qualia *do* seem to cause our actions. I.e., if I burn my hand on a stove, I snatch it away because of the pain. If we have a conversation about my feelings, my feelings *caused* that conversation.

So- do qualia have direct causal power over and above strictly physical dynamics, or do they not?

<u>Possible flavors of additional causal power:</u>
Computationalism lacks a concrete hypothesis about what qualia are, and thus how they could have causal power. However, there's generally a nod toward concepts such as "strong emergence" and "downward causation" in this context. As David Chalmers defines these terms,
> We can say that a high-level phenomenon is **strongly emergent** with respect to a low-level domain when the high-level phenomenon arises from the low-level domain, but truths concerning that phenomenon are not deducible even in principle from truths in the low-level domain.

---

[49] My prediction is that progress on each of these problems will only be made insofar as computationalism & IIT adopt the formalisms of physics. E.g., the Church-Turing-Deutsch (CTD) Principle suggests that a quantum computer could likely simulate a physical system perfectly- but at that point we're merely using physics to simulate physics. Furthermore, the CTD Principle as applied to *consciousness* doesn't address the issue that simulation is not necessarily identity. I.e., the Substrate Problem is still a problem.

> **Downward causation** means that higher-level phenomena are not only irreducible but also exert a causal efficacy of some sort. ... [This implies] low-level laws will be incomplete as a guide to both the low-level and the high-level evolution of processes in the world. (Chalmers 2008) (emphasis added)

Such definitions don't define a mechanism for how these ideas would work, and perhaps that's the point- if strongly emergent or downwardly causative phenomena exist, then we *can't* apply the sort of reduction that could extract a core mechanism. Because of this, there's a bit of mysticism surrounding such arguments.

Against downward causation:

The best- and perhaps only- way to fully disprove the possibility of downward causation would be to explain all extant phenomena without reference to it. But in the meantime, I think we should view it as a hypothesis of last resort, since (1) it doesn't explain anything, and merely says that some things are inherently inexplicable; and (2) it seems to directly contradict core tenets of modern physics. Here's Sean Carroll on how there doesn't seem to be any room for downward causation in the Standard Model:

> I really do think that enormous confusion is caused in many areas — not just consciousness, but free will and even more purely physical phenomena — by the simple mistake of starting sentences in one language or layer of description ("I thought about summoning up the will power to resist that extra slice of pizza...") but then ending them in a completely different vocabulary ("... but my atoms obeyed the laws of the Standard Model, so what could I do?") The dynamical rules of the Core Theory aren't just vague suggestions; they are absolutely precise statements about how the quantum fields making up you and me behave under any circumstances (within the "everyday life" domain of validity). And those rules say that the behavior of, say, an electron is determined by the local values of other quantum fields at the position of the electron — and by nothing else. (That's "locality" or "microcausality" in quantum field theory.) In particular, as long as the quantum fields at the precise position of the electron are the same, the larger context in which it is embedded is utterly irrelevant. (Carroll 2016).

What *is* happening when we talk about our qualia?

If 'downward causation' isn't real, then how *are* our qualia causing us to act? I suggest that we should look for solutions which describe why we have the *sensory illusion* of qualia having causal power, without actually adding another causal entity to the universe.

I believe this is much more feasible than it seems if we carefully examine the exact sense in which language is 'about' qualia. Instead of a direct representational interpretation, I offer we should instead think of language's 'aboutness' as a function of systematic correlations between two things *related to* qualia: the brain's *logical* state (i.e., connectome-level neural activity), particularly those logical states relevant to its self-model, and the brain's *microphysical* state (i.e., what the quarks which constitute the brain are doing).

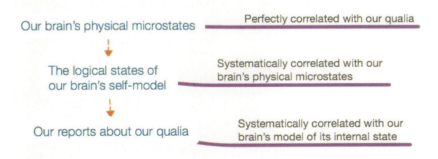

Our qualia, and our behavior & reports about our qualia, are not directly causally connected. Instead, they are connected more loosely through indirect systematic correlations. This implies that self-reports are not the "gold standard ground-truth" about qualia.

Our brain's physical microstates —— Perfectly correlated with our qualia

↓

The logical states of our brain's self-model —— Systematically correlated with our brain's physical microstates

↓

Our reports about our qualia —— Systematically correlated with our brain's model of its internal state

In short, our brain has evolved to be able to fairly accurately report its internal computational states (since it was adaptive to be able to coordinate such states with others), and these computational states are *highly correlated* with the microphysical states of the substrate the brain's computations run on (the actual source of qualia). However, these computational states and microphysical states are *not identical.* Thus, we would need to be open to the possibility that certain interventions could cause a change in a system's *physical* substrate (which generates its qualia) without causing a change in its *computational* level (which generates its qualia reports). We've evolved toward having our qualia, and our reports about our qualia, being synchronized- but in contexts where there *hasn't* been an adaptive pressure to accurately report our qualia, we shouldn't expect these to be synchronized 'for free'.

The details of precisely how our reports of qualia, and our ground-truth qualia, might diverge will greatly depend on what the actual physical substrate of consciousness is.[50] What is clear from this, however, is that transplanting the brain to a new substrate- e.g., emulating a human brain as software, on a traditional Von Neumann architecture computer- would likely produce qualia very different from the original, even if the high-level behavioral dynamics which generate its qualia reports were faithfully replicated. Copying qualia *reports* will likely not copy *qualia*.

I realize this notion that we could (at least in theory) be mistaken about what qualia we report & remember having is difficult to swallow. I would just say that although it may seem far-fetched, I think it's a necessary implication of all theories of qualia that don't resort to anti-scientific mysticism or significantly contradict what we know of physical laws.

Back to the question: why *do* we have the illusion that qualia have causal power?
In short, I'd argue that the brain is a complex, chaotic, coalition-based dynamic system with well-defined attractors and a high level of criticality (low activation energy needed to switch between attractors) that has an internal model of self-as-agent, yet can't predict itself. And I think *any* conscious system with these dynamics will have the quale of free will, and have the phenomenological illusion that its qualia have causal power.

And although it would be perfectly feasible for there to exist conscious systems which *don't* have the quale of free will, it's plausible that this quale will be relatively *common* across most evolved organisms. (Brembs 2011) argues that the sort of dynamical unpredictability which leads to the illusion of free will tends to be adaptive, both as a search strategy for hidden resources and as a game-theoretic advantage against predators, prey, and conspecifics: "[p]redictability can never be an evolutionarily stable strategy."

Appendix D: Remarks on the State Space Problem
"What is 'Qualia space'? - I.e., which precise mathematical object does the mathematical object isomorphic to a system's qualia live in? What are its structures/properties?

Anything we can figure out about the State Space Problem will give us tools for understanding the nature of qualia. So- what kind of problem is this? Here's Max Tegmark's Figure 12.1 from Our Mathematical Universe (Tegmark 2014a):

---

[50] Barrett's FIIH becomes both more plausible, and a lot weirder, under this assumption.

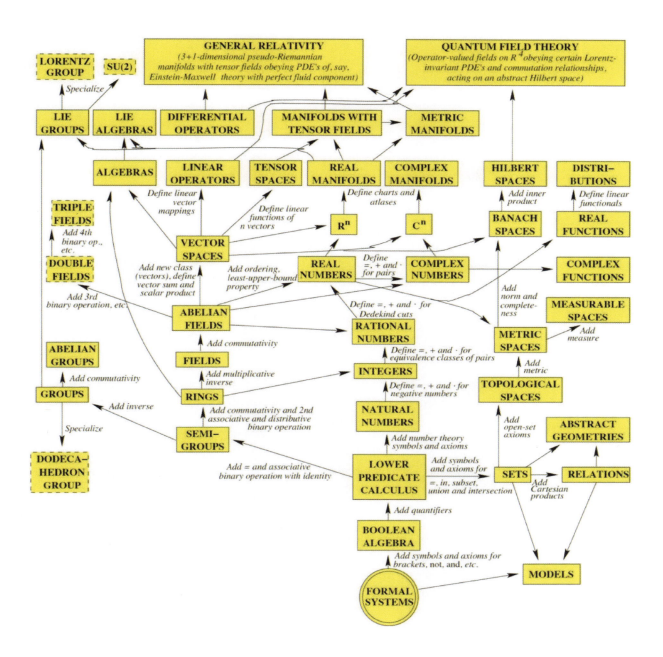

"Figure 12.1: Relationships between various basic mathematical structures. The arrows generally indicate addition of new symbols and/or axioms. Arrows that meet indicate the combination of structures--for instance, an algebra is a vector space that's also a ring, and a Lie group is a group that's also a manifold. The full family tree is probably infinite in extent--the figure shows merely a small sample near the bottom."

Presumably a "data structure isomorphic to the phenomenology of a system" is native to, or 'lives in' exactly one such mathematical structure.

Qualia space's mathematical structures:

Mathematicians classify mathematical objects based on which properties they embody- these properties are labeled 'structures'. Examples of structures include being able to multiply and add elements (->algebraic structure), or a formal notion of 'distance' between points (->metric structure), or combinations such as having a metric structure and also being mathematically 'flat' (->Euclidean geometric structure).

Previously, we noted that Qualia space probably has a topology (it probably has properties such as *connectedness* and *compactness*), and may be a metric space, since:
(a) IIT's output format is data in a vector space,
(b) Physics models reality as a wave function within Hilbert Space, which has substantial structure,
(c) Components of phenomenology such as color behave as vectors (Feynman 1965), and
(d) Spatial awareness is explicitly geometric.
These aren't *proof* of anything yet, but are suggestive that we can speak of *distances* within Qualia space.

Which other mathematical structures might Qualia space embody? The book has yet to be written here, but I expect it to have a fairly rich set of structures- comparable, perhaps, to the Hilbert Space which describes most of modern physics, since if we assume physicalism, there will be mappings or projections between the state space of qualia and the state spaces of the rest of physics.

Qualia space's symmetries & invariances:

We've already hypothesized that the *overall geometric symmetry* of the specific mathematical object isomorphic to a given phenomenology should correspond to its *valence*- but we may be able to wring more out of the study of the symmetries of the space it lives in.

Specifically, let's look to Noether's theorem, which states that for every symmetry in the mathematical structure which describes our laws of physics, there will be a conserved (invariant) quantity in our physical reality (Noether 1918). This applies to systems whose equations result from varying a Lagrangian or Hamiltonian-- i.e., all of modern physics.

Here again is Tegmark (Chapter 12, Our Mathematical Universe) describing how this cashes out in physics:
> The German mathematician Emmy Noether proved in 1915 that **each continuous symmetry of our mathematical structure leads to a so-called conservation law of physics, whereby some quantity is guaranteed to stay constant**--and thereby have the sort of permanence that might make self-aware observers take note of it and give it a "baggage" name. All the conserved quantities that we discussed in Chapter 7 correspond to such symmetries: for example, energy corresponds to time-translation symmetry (that our laws of physics stay the same for all time), momentum corresponds to space-translation symmetry (that the laws are the same everywhere), angular momentum corresponds to rotation symmetry (that empty space has no special "up" direction) and electric charge corresponds to a certain symmetry of quantum mechanics. The Hungarian physicist Eugene Wigner went on to show that these symmetries also dictated all the quantum properties that particles can have, including mass and spin. In other words, between the two of them, Noether and Wigner showed that, at least in our own mathematical structure, studying the symmetries reveals what sort of "stuff" can exist in it. As I mentioned in Chapter 7, some physics colleagues of mine with a penchant for math jargon like to quip that a particle is simply "an element of an irreducible representation of the symmetry group." It's become clear that practically all our laws of physics originate in symmetries, and the physics Nobel laureate Philip Warren Anderson has gone even further, saying, **"It is only slightly overstating the case to say that physics is the study of symmetry."** [Emphasis added.] (Tegmark 2014a)

Does this *also* apply to *qualia*? Lacking a firm mathematical foundation for qualia, we must speculate, but it seems reasonable & generative to predict that symmetries in the mathematical object which defines Qualia space should correspond to conserved properties/relationships in *qualia*, and vice-versa. To re-state this:

"Let's look for conserved properties like energy or momentum, or the SU(3)×SU(2)×U(1) gauge symmetries, but for qualia."

Global symmetries vs local symmetries: In physics, 'global' symmetries are invariances which hold uniformly throughout the system, and produce conservation laws. Examples include conservation of energy, linear momentum, and angular momentum. 'Local' symmetries can be thought of as equivalence classes which define allowable transformations in the state space, and produce forces. Examples include gravity, electromagnetism, and the strong and weak forces.

Class	Invariance	Conserved quantity
Proper orthochronous Lorentz symmetry	translation in time (homogeneity)	energy
	translation in space (homogeneity)	linear momentum
	rotation in space (isotropy)	angular momentum
Discrete symmetry	P, coordinate inversion	spatial parity
	C, charge conjugation	charge parity
	T, time reversal	time parity
	CPT	product of parities
Internal symmetry (independent of spacetime coordinates)	U(1) gauge transformation	electric charge
	U(1) gauge transformation	lepton generation number
	U(1) gauge transformation	hypercharge
	U(1)$_Y$ gauge transformation	weak hypercharge
	U(2) [U(1) × SU(2)]	electroweak force
	SU(2) gauge transformation	isospin
	SU(2)$_L$ gauge transformation	weak isospin
	P × SU(2)	G-parity
	SU(3) "winding number"	baryon number
	SU(3) gauge transformation	quark color
	SU(3) (approximate)	quark flavor

Table from Wikipedia: fundamental symmetries and their associated conserved quantities.

What would the phenomenology of conserved properties in Qualia space be? It's hard to say anything firmly at this point, but we can speculate:

Phenomenology of global symmetries: all qualia seems to obey *time translation symmetry* (the laws of qualia don't change over time), which if this line of thinking is right, should correspond to a global symmetry of Qualia space. In physics, time translation symmetry leads to conservation of energy; in qualia, perhaps this shows up in a different-but-weirdly-similar form. Similarly, consciousness seems invariant under translation and rotation in space, so we should look for phenomenological analogues of linear & angular momentum.

Phenomenology of local symmetries: the different 'flavors' of gluons which mediate the Strong Nuclear Force obey certain conservation laws due to local symmetry, and their charge was named 'color charge' precisely because its state space behaves like the state space of colors. Brian Flanagan suggests that we should consider this similarity less metaphorically and more literally: "it is as though each speck in the visual field is tangent to color space — as though a color sphere "sits over" each spacetime coordinate of the visual field, in direct analogy with string/M-theory and Kaluza-Klein theory." (Flanagan 2007)[51] We may be able to work backward from the state space & dynamics of color to a *local symmetry* in Qualia space.

More generally, we should keep an eye out for qualia *like* colors and valence which seem to vary within a well-defined state space. Wittgenstein notes this is a common phenomenon: "a speck in the visual field, though it need not be red must have some color; it is, so to speak, surrounded by color-space. Notes must have some pitch, objects of the sense of touch some degree of hardness, and so on". (Wittgenstein 1922)

How easy will it be to find invariants/symmetries in Qualia space? We can recall Tegmark's passage above, which suggests that conserved quantities may have already found their way into our language, since they're stable reference points- a point originally made by Wigner (E. Wigner 1967). But we can also consider that invariants/symmetries in Qualia space are so familiar and simple that we ignore them: as Wittgenstein notes, "The aspects of things that are most important for us are hidden because of their simplicity and familiarity. (One is unable to notice something because it is always before one's eyes.) The real foundations of his enquiry do not strike a man at all." (Wittgenstein 1953) This blindness-to-obvious-things is probably the *most* true when we're speaking of invariant patterns in qualia, since it seems plausible that evolution has optimized our attention *away* from spending cognitive resources on noticing invariants, because there is no adaptive benefit in doing so.[52]

Andres Gomez Emilsson notes that psychedelic states may be particularly useful in elucidating such invariant relationships in Qualia space by rapidly exposing us to new combinations and giving us fresh eyes for existing patterns:
> To the extent that psychedelic states enable the exploration of a larger space of possible experiences, we are more likely while on psychedelics to find states of consciousness that demonstrate fundamental limits imposed by the structure of the state-space of qualia. In normal everyday experience we can see that yellow and blue cannot be mixed (phenomenologically), while yellow and red can (and thus deliver orange). This being a constraint of the state-space of qualia itself is not at all evident, but it is a good candidate and many introspective individuals agree. On psychedelic states one can detect many other rules like that, except that they operate on much higher-dimensional and synesthetic spaces (E.g. "Some feelings of roughness and tinges of triangle orange can mix well, while some spiky mongrels and blue halos simply won't touch no matter how much I try." – 150 micrograms of LSD). (Gomez Emilsson 2016)

---

[51] Flanagan goes further, and implies that this might imply color has something to do with gauge particles *directly*. This seems to be pure speculation and I'm skeptical-- but frankly, we need more definite, falsifiable hypotheses in qualia research.
[52] Furthermore, it's important to note that on top of *these* problems with language's inexactness and blind spots, there's an additional problem that we may not be able to trust self-reports as 'qualia ground truth' (see Appendix C).

Naturally, any progress in locating the Standard Model as part of a more fundamental unified structure[53] would make the State Space Problem easier. Likewise, progress on the State Space Problem could lead to hints on how to generalize the Standard Model.

Appendix E: Remarks on the Substrate Problem
"Which subset of objects & processes in our chosen ontology [in this case, physics] 'count' toward consciousness?"

The Substrate Problem is the second-most foundational problem in consciousness research, upstream of everything but the Reality Mapping Problem, so it's very important.

However, making progress on the Substrate Problem has also proven very *difficult*, for several reasons:
  (1) *No clear data to guide us*: We have some knowledge about the macro-causal conditions that give rise to consciousness (e.g., the data & arguments marshalled by Tononi et al. about integration), but none fine-grained enough to tease apart what this data means and what's correlated with it at the 'basement' physical level, and which abstractions to bring to bear on the problem;
  (2) *Non-physicists tend to stumble on the Reality Mapping Problem*: people tend to approach consciousness with the toolsets they're familiar with- e.g., neuroscientists think of neurons, computer scientists think of computation, and so on. If consciousness *is* a physics problem, this diverts a lot of effort into cul-de-sacs which *at best* can only ever be *inspirational templates* for a more correct *physical* theory (see Appendix C);
  (3) *Few physicists work on consciousness*: with a few exceptions, research on the physics of consciousness is generally seen as the playground of crackpots and/or something to do at the end of a long, traditional, "safe" career in physics. Uncareful, pseudo-scientific claims connecting weird aspects of quantum mechanics with strange things about consciousness are distressingly common, and the omnipresent threat of 'pattern-matching to crackpot' makes consciousness research a minefield for physicists who value their professional reputations;
  (4) *Having to choose between incompatible interpretations of phenomena such as time and decoherence creates theoretical silos*: the more interpretive choices a theory of consciousness must make, the smaller the body of literature it will be compatible with.
  (5) *The Scale Problem is really hard to address with physics*: the scales that fundamental physical processes occur at are very small (anstroms) and fast (femtoseconds). The scales that consciousness seems to occur at are much larger (neuron-scale?) and slower (hundreds of milliseconds). It's unclear how to bridge this gap in both an *elegant* and *plausible* way;
  (6) *Confusion about what a "theory of consciousness" needs to do:* perhaps the most serious issue is that there's widespread confusion over what consciousness is, what a successful solution to consciousness would look like, and how questions of substrate feed into other subproblems (see Figure 6).

There is no consensus on what the physical substrate of consciousness is; insofar as they *are* formalized, few would even grant that any of the current crop of hypotheses *could* be correct. It's a rather dismal research landscape.

However, some patterns do emerge when we look at physical theorists who have been brave (or foolhardy) enough to throw their hats into the ring:

---

[53] Progress on the *holographic principle* (the idea that spacetime is a projection of a lower-dimensional object- or more generally, that the most elegant way to understand a region of spacetime is through theory defined on the region's boundary, not its interior) could be generative also. And we should keep an eye out for *direct* applications of the holographic principle to qualia and the State Space Problem.

Orch-OR: Roger Penrose & Stuart Hameroff emphasize how consciousness is embedded within time, change, and computation with their focus on the collapse of the wavefunction. According to their theory of Orchestrated Objective Reduction (Orch-OR), consciousness is what it feels like to be a quantum computer choosing which states to decohere into.

However, Orch-OR is generally viewed with skepticism on both physical and philosophical grounds. Physically, there seems to be little evidence for its biological plausibility-- in particular, the brain seems much too 'warm, wet, and noisy' to prevent decoherence on the order of femtoseconds (Tegmark 2000), which would prevent quantum processes from meaningfully interacting with neuron-scale events. Philosophically, Penrose's rationale for defining the mind *as* a quantum computer is that 'because humans are capable of knowing the truth of Gödel-unprovable statements, human thought is necessarily non-computable' (the Penrose-Lucas argument). However, as widely noted by critics, it's unclear that defining the mind as a quantum computer is either necessary or sufficient to address this problem, and the problem (and rationale for Orch-OR) may thus instead rest on bad definitions.

Historically, consciousness was seen as somehow necessary for performing measurements that would lead to a collapse of the wave function (the "von Neumann–Wigner interpretation", and similar work by David Bohm). Orch-OR is the most nuanced version- and one of the last outposts- of this philosophy.

Perceptronium: Max Tegmark uses information theory and anthropic reasoning to offer some constraints on how IIT-like integration could be formalized in terms of quantum theory with his 'Perceptronium' paper (Tegmark 2015). It's a masterwork smörgåsbord of anthropic reasoning about conscious systems, mathematical exploration of types & degrees of integration in quantum physics, and various other topics that might be relevant to the physics of consciousness. However, it's not actually a theory *per se*, and is silent on what the actual substrate of consciousness *is*. (I review more details of Tegmark's work in Section V.)

FIIH: Adam Barrett emphasizes the ontological primacy of fields in quantum mechanics in his suggestion that we should build something like IIT out of quantum field theory. His 'field integrated information hypothesis' (FIIH) is an intriguing idea that straddles two very important notions. However, it also suffers from two significant flaws: (1) it's not actually formalized yet, and (2) it has no empirical support- and a ready counterexample, since electromagnetic fields don't seem to influence our qualia reports, *at all*. However, we shouldn't throw it out just because it violates our expectation that changes in qualia should always be reportable: a physics approach to consciousness *does seem to imply* that system behavior (reports of qualia) may not always covary with system qualia. Instead, *we should only expect evolved systems to be able to faithfully report their qualia in ways and contexts that have been evolutionarily advantageous to do so*. And this counter-intuitive fact may be true of *any* fully-quantitative theory of consciousness. (I cover more details of Barrett's work in Section V, and the topic of qualia reports in Appendix C.)

Scott Aaronson emphasizes irreversibility & unpredictability with his suggestion that systems must "participate fully in the arrow of time", or continually undergo irreversible decoherence, as a necessary condition for being conscious (Aaronson 2014b; Aaronson 2016). It's a novel idea that solves several problems with one move- e.g., no reversible process could be conscious, so there would be no way to 'uncompute' qualia. Likewise, only processes that are basically impossible to predict could be conscious, so this would rescue some version of Free Will. And it's plausible that decoherence *is* ontologically fundamental, and participation in the arrow of time is metaphysically important.

However, there's a question of whether "irreversible decoherence" has a definition which is both *crisp* and *plausible* for forming a basis for consciousness. Aaronson doesn't bill this as a complete theory of consciousness, just as one requirement among others, and as he notes, it involves some counter-intuitive notions:

> [A]m I saying that, in order to be absolutely certain of whether some entity satisfied the postulated precondition for consciousness, one might, in general, need to look billions of years into the future, to see

whether the "decoherence" produced by the entity was really irreversible? Yes (pause to gulp bullet). I am saying that.

David Pearce emphasizes the unitary nature of consciousness with his notion that complex conscious states require quantum coherence to 'bind' micro-experiences together. This view parallels Orch-OR in some ways- it implies that the mind is a quantum computer- but focuses on *coherence* rather than *decoherence*. The core of Pearce's argument is that consciousness is "ontologically unitary", and so only a physical property that implies ontological unity (such as quantum coherence) could physically instantiate consciousness. As an intuitive effort to connect these two things Pearce's work is a notable landmark, but it's not particularly formalized at this time.[54]

This is a partial and highly idiosyncratic list of theories. And unfortunately, the landscape for possible solutions to the Substrate Problem is large and any given theory is very unlikely to be true. Without tight falsification loops, this makes it difficult to make progress.

But there aren't infinite degrees of freedom for building theories of consciousness, and if we can *parametrize* the explanation space, we can approach it *systematically*, and also move toward a more modular approach where we can mix-and-match assumptions, tools, and formalisms. I suggest three techniques here:

1. Constraining the Substrate Problem by linking it to other problems:

First, the fact that the Substrate Problem feeds into other problems can help us evaluate theories' potential and completeness. I.e., a theorist can assert that "X is the substrate for consciousness", but we should strongly prefer statement such as "X is the substrate for consciousness, which means the Boundary & Scale Problems get solved for free because of Y, and this implies Z about the Topology of Information Problem."

2. Parametrizing the Substrate Problem by looking at physics:

Second, based on the assumption that consciousness "has to be hiding somewhere" within fundamental physics, we can attempt to look for it systematically by looking at each component of physics ('physics-as-axiomatic-system') and check which fundamental entities, processes, or interactions we can build plausible theories of consciousness from.

I.e.: can we use the formalisms of quantum entanglement to build something like IIT's notion of 'integrated information' at plausible scales? What about quantum field theory (as Barrett suggests)? Essentially, if there are N fundamental entities in quantum theory, we can just go down the list and try to build plausible formalisms for each. It'd be *hard* and *painstaking* work, but not impossible.

3. Parametrizing the Substrate Problem by looking at consciousness:

Finally, we can also look at what sort of thing we think consciousness *is*, and try to find plausible matches in physics. I'd identify the following core decision points:

1. *Static vs dynamic*: should we think of consciousness as inherently arising from certain arrangements of particles, or from the change (i.e., dynamic interactions) which happens *between* each arrangement?
   - If consciousness is linked to change, is this sort of change *reversible* or *irreversible*?

2. *Anthropics:* is our way of experiencing physical dynamics & the arrow of time the only way possible, or (as Tegmark suggests), are there many factorizations of the wave function which could support consciousness?

---

[54] Matthew Fisher has put forth a creative yet untested mechanism which might be able to physically ground this model based on entangled spins of phosphorus atoms (Fisher 2015).

3. *Binding prerequisites*: does the substrate of consciousness require some special property which can support "ontological unity" (e.g., Pearce's focus on quantum coherence) to bind together 'micro-experiences', or should we focus on information-theoretic aggregation techniques (e.g., IIT's Minimum Information Partition)?

This list of decision points is very provisional and certainly non-exhaustive. But if we can identify N decision points, we can split up the problem space into 2^n possibilities and work through them.

Let's drop down a level and attempt to give an example use of this sort of framework. So-- to pick a few options semi-arbitrarily, let's assume we're looking for a theory of consciousness based on a *dynamic* phenomenon which is *irreversible*, and that addresses the Boundary/Binding Problem similar to how IIT does. *What could this look like?*

Example hypothesis: the Maximum Branching Decoherence Partition (MBDP), a mash-up of Giulio Tononi's IIT and Scott Aaronson's decoherence hypothesis that could address the Substrate, Boundary, and Scale Problems:

IIT solves the 'Boundary Problem', or how to draw the boundaries of a conscious system, and the 'Scale Problem', or the spatial & temporal scale by which to measure this partition, via the concept of a Minimum Information Partition (MIP): given a set of interacting components, the partition of the system (and the spatial & temporal *scale* of the partition) which 'counts' is the one that minimizes the ratio of nodes-to-integrated-information.

Physicalists need a similarly principled way to solve these problems, but built out of fundamental physics, and I think Aaronson's thoughts on decoherence may give us a means of doing so while also re-using most of IIT's framework.

<u>*Decoherence: enemy of consciousness, or friend?*</u>

In his Perceptronium paper, Tegmark suggested that decoherence is something that conscious systems should *minimize* (or at least *neutralize*), in order to preserve system autonomy and predictability, which are requirements for intelligent behavior: "for a conscious system to be able to predict the future state of what it cares about (ρ_o) as well as possible, we must minimize uncertainty introduced both by the interactions with the environment (fluctuation, dissipation and decoherence) and by measurement ("quantum randomness")." (Tegmark 2015)

However, Aaronson (Aaronson 2014b; Aaronson 2016) suggests the *exact opposite*: in addition to other factors, decoherence may be a <u>*necessary condition*</u> for consciousness:

> "[Y]es, consciousness is a property of any suitably-organized chunk of matter. But, in addition to performing complex computations, or passing the Turing Test, or other information-theoretic conditions that I don't know (and don't claim to know), there's at least one crucial further thing that a chunk of matter has to do before we should consider it conscious. Namely, **it has to participate fully in the Arrow of Time**. More specifically, it has to produce irreversible decoherence as an intrinsic part of its operation. It has to be continually taking microscopic fluctuations, and irreversibly amplifying them into stable, copyable, macroscopic classical records.
> …
> So, why might one conjecture that decoherence, and participation in the arrow of time, were necessary conditions for consciousness? I suppose I could offer some argument about our subjective experience of the passage of time being a crucial component of our consciousness, and the passage of time being bound up with the Second Law. Truthfully, though, I don't have any a-priori argument that I find convincing. All I can do is show you how many apparent paradoxes get resolved if you make this one speculative leap." [Emphasis in original.]

Aaronson goes on to list some paradoxes and puzzling edge-cases that resolve if 'full participation in the Arrow of Time' is a necessary condition for a system being consciousness: e.g., whether brains which have undergone Fully Homomorphic Encryption (FHE) could still be conscious (no- Aaronson suggests that nothing with a clean digital abstraction layer could be) or whether a fully-reversible quantum computer could exhibit consciousness (no- Aaronson argues that no fully-reversible process could be).

This gets especially interesting if we view decoherence and integration as intimately related properties: it seems plausible that systems that fulfill Aaronson's criteria "that *microscopic* decoherence fluctuations are irreversibly amplified into *macroscopic* records" will necessarily be highly integrated, and if we were to formally calculate the branching decoherence occurring within a physical system, the math we'd use would likely have many parallels with how IIT calculates integrated information. This leads to the following: Aaronson argues that decoherence is *necessary* for consciousness. Could it also be *sufficient*?

Essentially, we could reimagine IIT's *Minimum Information Partition* (the partition of a system which minimizes the ratio of nodes-to-integrated-information) in terms of quantum decoherence. We could call this the *Maximum Branching Partition* (MBP), or the 4D partition of a system which defines a local maximum in branching (MW interpretation) decoherence rate[55]. The scalar measure of the partition's 'total branching distance' from the starting state, which we can call Φ^D, thus constitutes the *degree of consciousness* of the system and takes the place of IIT's Φ. One way to think about this quantity would be the *amount of irreversibility* involved in the partition's quantum evolution, and we could use some sort of earth mover's distance (or adapt Yao's quantum circuit complexity?) to compute this. (A good *intuitive* proxy for Φ^D would be the amount of negentropy a partition of space-time has burned, though this is a somewhat less precise quantity.)

Promisingly, since integration and decoherence are interestingly coupled, and since we're reusing IIT's method of partitioning space-time based on the local maximum of some property, we can re-use most of IIT's solutions to various problems. E.g., groups of neurons and hundreds of milliseconds should be the scales that contribute the most when calculating the MBP for reasons very similar to why Tononi believes neurons and milliseconds contribute the most to IIT's MIP, and we can re-use most of IIT's framework for constructing a mathematical object 'isomorphic to the phenomenology of a conscious system' based on causal clustering.

	Estimated rate of irreversible (branching) decoherence:
Brain: 1ns	Little, since small fluctuations haven't had time to get amplified
Brain: 200ms	Large, since this is the scale which maximizes system criticality
Brain: 10m	Moderate, since it averages the peaks and troughs of decoherence rate over time
Digital computer	Tiny, since the long-term effects of small fluctuations are actively suppressed
Ice Cube	Little, since small fluctuations have no mechanism for amplification

If such a formalism could be found, the result would be an IIT-style theory which is firmly based in quantum mechanics, seemingly consistent with Tegmark's six principles for Perceptronium, and also satisfying Aaronson's notion that conscious systems must 'participate fully in the arrow of time'[56]. Some of the details of how I've expressed it are ambiguous, and others could be wrong, but this general approach seems a viable way forward for Perceptronium or (Orch-OR).

---

[55] Most likely, this is compatible with other decoherence interpretations- e.g., wave function collapse.
[56] If at some point we can build the passage of time out of a stochastic process involving decoherence (personal correspondence, Giego Caleiro), tying consciousness to decoherence gets even more compelling.

	IIT 3.0	Tegmark's Perceptronium hypothesis	Aaronson's decoherence hypothesis	Orch-OR	Global Workspace Theory	MBDP Theory
Has a principled way to draw the boundaries of a conscious system	X			X		X
Proposes a mechanism to calculate the degree of consciousness of a system	X	X				X
Proposes a mechanism to calculate the qualia a system is experiencing	X					X
Fully formalized	X					
Has a principled way to apply at the scales of neurons & milliseconds	X				X	X
Has zero ambiguity in how to apply it to arbitrary physical systems		X				X
Deals with reversible quantum computation & encrypted minds in a principled way			X			X
Predictions & interpretations consistent with mainstream science	X	X	X		X	X

Table: desirable properties of theories of consciousness, and an optimistic *extrapolation* of how this *style* of hypothesis could stack up against other options if we 'turn the crank' on each theory. Note that MBDP theory is *not* formalized at this time.

Just to be clear- this is an example of how to use my parametrization of the Substrate Problem to generate hypotheses. I do think this *sort* of thinking may prove fruitful, and this specific hypothesis *could* be correct, but it would be unreasonable to put much weight on any given unformalized & unproven hypothesis.

Appendix F: Some Cosmological Musings

My core arguments about valence & consciousness have long concluded. But before I sign off, permit me to offer the loyal readers who have gotten this far a larger perspective on these topics, and to float an admittedly odd (but possibly important) notion.

A cosmological perspective:

We tend to think of consciousness, and theories of consciousness, on a *human* scale. This seems reasonable, since it's the only context for consciousness that we know anything about. But if we aim to have a well-defined, truly frame-invariant understanding of consciousness, we need to bite the bullet and accept that it should apply equally at non-human scales as well.

But things get strange very quickly when we consider theories of consciousness such as IIT, Perceptronium, and my MBDP Theory at *cosmological* scales. Humanity seems to think that they are the lone candle of consciousness, flickering in the surrounding void of inert matter-- but what if the opposite is true? I submit it would be *surprisingly difficult* to fully-formalize a plausible theory of consciousness where the biological life of Earth constitutes the majority of the universe's qualia.

Where else could qualia be found, if not humans? List your preferred frame-invariant condition for consciousness (integrated information, decoherence, "complexity", etc), then consider how much of this consciousness-stuff the following cosmological phenomena might have:

The Big Bang: presumably, packing everything in our observable universe into an area smaller than an electron would have produced an *incredible* amount of integration (etc) with *incredibly* fine spatial & temporal grain. So much so that it seems plausible that >99.9% of the universe's total qualia (in a *timeless* sense) could have happened within its first ~hour.

To put this poetically- **perhaps we are qualia godshatter, slowly recoalescing ~14 billion years after the main event**.

Eternal Inflation: inflationary cosmology- the idea that the early universe underwent an exponential expansion during the Big Bang- is "an ingenious attempt to solve some of the major puzzles of cosmology, most notably the flatness problem, the homogeneity (horizon) problem, and the monopole problem." (Penrose 1989) First proposed in the

1980s, it's still considered the best hypothesis we have for understanding why our universe has the distribution of mass & geometry it does.

An important implication of the inflation model is that, due to the math involved, it never quite *stops*. Sean Carroll notes that:

> [M]ost — "essentially all" — models of inflation lead to the prediction that inflation never completely ends. The vicissitudes of quantum fluctuations imply that even inflation doesn't smooth out everything perfectly. As a result, inflation will end in some places, but in other places it keeps going. Where it keeps going, space expands at a fantastic rate. In some parts of that region, inflation eventually ends, but in others it keeps going. And that process continues forever, with some part of the universe perpetually undergoing inflation. That's how the multiverse gets off the ground — we're left with a chaotic jumble consisting of numerous "pocket universes" separated by regions of inflating spacetime. (Carroll 2011)

If this eternal inflation model of the universe is right, this inflationary process is almost certainly creating an *infinite* amount of qualia.

Our Future: it seems possible that- if we don't kill ourselves first- our future could hold much more consciousness than the present. Kurzweil puts this possibility as "*The Universe Wakes Up*" and becomes conscious, thanks to our intervention.

Planck Scale phenomena: Perhaps the virtual particles continually popping in and out of existence in a quantum vacuum, or a quantum vacuum itself, involve a very small amount of integrated information. There's a *lot* of stuff happening at the Planck Scale, so if it generates *any* qualia, it would be a huge amount of *total* qualia.

Megastructures: what would it feel like to be a black hole? Are black holes Bose-Einstein condensates, and if so does that imply anything about their qualia or their ability to store&process information? Is there any integrated information in a quasar?[57] We don't generally talk about megastructures as having complex structure, but that may just be limitations on our models & measurements.

Partitions of reality we can't see: as Max Tegmark notes in his Perceptronium paper, we experience a certain partition of Hilbert Space as reality. He argues that there might be other partitions of Hilbert Space that could support consciousness, too. Likewise, there may be other multiverses (Levels I, II, III, and IV, in Tegmark's framework) that support consciousness. And so it seems easily possible that the majority of qualia being generated is outside of our particular partition and/or multiverse.

The above comments likely come across as a type error: *'black holes can't be conscious, and it couldn't have felt like anything to be the Big Bang- don't be ridiculous!'* - but, I would challenge those who would object to explain *why* in a formal way. As noted above, I think we'd be hard-pressed to define a fully frame-invariant theory of consciousness where the above sorts of cosmological events *wouldn't* involve consciousness. So I think we have to bite the bullet here.

Finally, I end with some low-probability (<10%) speculation that I won't ask my readers to bite the bullet on. I offer the following less as an argument, and more as an optimistic- and somewhat whimsical- exploration.

---

[57] Cosmology has put a lot of effort into studying "standard candles", or stars which have a precisely predictable energy output due to transitions which happen at precisely known mass thresholds. Is the qualia-relevant microstructure of standard candles also similar across a given class? E.g., do all type Ia supernovae *feel* fairly similar?

Hypothesis: many of these cosmological events may involve high- and sometimes *extreme*- amounts of symmetry. *Status: unrepentantly speculative. Dependent upon many nested assumptions.*

We can now move on to the next sort of question: "if it felt like something to be the Big Bang, what did it feel *like*?"; "if a black hole *has* qualia, what qualia *does* it have?

Obviously, I don't know the answer. But some of these cosmological events are notable for having an *extreme degree of symmetry*, which- if my hypothesis is correct- means they should feel *pretty good*.

The Big Bang & Eternal Inflation are probably the best understood example of a high-symmetry cosmological event. The rapid inflation of our universe, which cosmologists are fairly certain describes our past, *requires* an extremely low-entropy starting point in order to happen (something close to a de Sitter space, which is the 'maximally symmetric solution of Einstein's field equations with a positive cosmological constant'). There are huge unknowns here: e.g., is low-entropy here the same as high-symmetry? What is the measure we should use for symmetry-which-is-relevant-for-valence? *Why* did the universe start with such a low-entropy state to begin with? But the Big Bang probably had, and the ongoing Eternal Inflation probably has, an extremely high amount of whatever the symmetry relevant to valence is.

Also of note, Max Tegmark has suggested that the Many-Worlds interpretation of quantum mechanics may imply substantial symmetries that are 'hidden' from observers like us:
> [In the Level III multiverse] the quantum superposition of field configurations decoheres into what is for all practical purposes an ensemble of classical universes with different density fluctuation patterns. Just as in all cases of spontaneous symmetry breaking, the symmetry is never broken in the bird's view, merely in the frog's view: a translationally and rotationally quantum state (wave functional) such as the Bunch-Davies vacuum can decohere into an incoherent superposition of states that lack any symmetry. (Tegmark 2007)

If these high-symmetry 'birds-eye views' of a Many Worlds reality can support qualia, and of course assuming my hypothesis about valence is correct, the qualia would plausibly be very pleasant.[58]

My point here is that there could be a *lot* of very pleasant qualia laying around, under certain not-implausible assumptions about consciousness and valence. Perhaps an *amazingly huge* amount.

Bostrom's Simulation Argument:

One last piece of the puzzle: Nick Bostrom's Simulation Argument (SA) suggests that at least some advanced civilizations will make universe simulations, and if they do, they will make *lots* of such simulations. This implies we are statistically likely to be living in a simulation. More technically, Bostrom argues that:
> [A]t least one of the following propositions is true: (1) the human species is very likely to go extinct before reaching a "posthuman" stage; (2) any posthuman civilization is extremely unlikely to run a significant number of simulations of their evolutionary history (or variations thereof); (3) we are almost certainly living in a computer simulation. (Bostrom 2003)

Bostrom's argument *as stated* relies on consciousness being substrate-independent: he assumes that "it would suffice for the generation of subjective experiences that the computational processes of a human brain are structurally replicated in suitably fine-grained detail, such as on the level of individual synapses." I think there are very good reasons to doubt this, as noted in Appendix C and (McCabe 2005).

---

[58] Likewise, Tegmark notes that different Level II multiverses can support "different ways in which space can be compactified, which can allow both different effective dimensionality and different symmetries/elementary articles (corresponding to different topology of the curled up extra dimensions)."

But I think Bostrom doesn't *need* this assumption of substrate-independence for his argument. I suggest the following middle ground: as Bostrom notes, we could be living in a simulation. But as McCabe argues, if we *are* in a simulation, it wouldn't really 'count' as being a *metaphysically separate* reality. Instead, we would simply be living in a weirdly-partitioned view of basement reality, since a simulation can't take on any strong emergent properties over and above the hardware it's being run on. Importantly, this means the *underlying physical rules* for consciousness would be the same for us as they would be for the entities running our simulations. But in practice, the simulation could *present* these rules to us very differently than they would be presented in unfiltered basement reality.

Why simulate anything?

At any rate, let's assume the simulation argument is viable- i.e., it's *possible* we're a simulation, and due to the anthropic math, that it's *plausible* that we're in one now.

Although it's possible that we are being simulated but for no reason, let's assume entities smart enough to simulate universes would have a good *reason* to do so. So- what possible good reason could there be to simulate a universe? Two options come to mind:
(a) using the evolution of the physical world to compute something, or
(b) something to do with qualia.

In theory, (a) could be tested by assuming that efficient computations will exhibit high degrees of Kolmogorov complexity (incompressibility) from certain viewpoints, and low Kolmogorov complexity from others. We could then formulate an anthropic-aware measure for this applicable from 'within' a computational system, and apply it to our observable universe. This is outside the scope of this work.

However, we *can* offer a suggestion about (b): if our universe is being simulated for some reason associated with qualia, it seems plausible that it has to do with producing a *large amount* of some kind of *particularly interesting* or *morally relevant* qualia. The one quale that seems *particularly* interesting and *especially* morally relevant[59] is positive valence.

--> Hypothesis: the universe could be being simulated to generate lots of positive valence. Let's call this the Teleologic Simulation for Valence (TSfV) Hypothesis. It implies that all contingent facts of our universe (e.g., all free variables in the Standard Model) are optimized for *maximizing total positive valence*.

Evidence/predictions for TSfV:

The way to test this would be exploring whether we live in a universe which seems *improbably* likely to support lots of positive valence, and if we can't explain contingent features of our universe *without* assuming this. I.e., can the TSfV hypothesis make successful predictions that mere anthropic reasoning *can't*? Likewise, if we can find a *single contingent physical constant* not optimized for the maximization of positive valence (more strictly, consciousness*valence*intensity, per Section X[60]), this would disprove the hypothesis.

The clearest argument *for* this TSfV hypothesis revolves around the initial low-entropy state (a 'quasi' de Sitter space) which allows Eternal Inflation. How this state came about is currently an unsolved problem in cosmology, and if it (or something upstream of it) *is* contingent and we can't explain it in any other way, this would be strong evidence. Here's Sean Carroll:

---

[59] I am not claiming valence is necessarily the only quale of moral relevance, merely that it is the quale that is most obviously morally relevant.
[60] E.g., we should look for optimization for high symmetry, but not *perfect* symmetry everywhere and everywhen, since this presumably wouldn't allow room for the sort of complexity which gives rise to consciousness (or the passage of time).

Although inflation does seem to create a universe like ours, it needs to start in a very particular kind of state. If the laws of physics are "unitary" (reversible, preserving information over time), then the number of states that would begin to inflate is actually much smaller than the number of states that just look like the hot Big Bang in the first place. So inflation seems to replace a fine-tuning of initial conditions with an even greater fine-tuning. (Carroll 2011)

Many other arguments could be made, particularly, surrounding the four other topics I identify above, but there are too many unknowns to say very much with confidence. Progress here will depend on better understanding the physical representation of the symmetry that 'matters' for valence, connecting this with various definitions of entropy, calculating expected qualia & valence of various cosmological events, and general progress on cosmological models.

Leibniz famously argued that we live in the best possible world, based on the following argument:

1. God has the idea of infinitely many universes.
2. Only one of these universes can actually exist.
3. God's choices are subject to the principle of sufficient reason, that is, God has reason to choose one thing or another.
4. God is good.
5. Therefore, the universe that God chose to exist is the best of all possible worlds. (Leibniz 1710 (1989))

This argument fell into disfavor due to the problems of evil and suffering, the triumph of evolution & empirical science over theology & reasoning from first-principles, and ambiguity over what makes a universe 'good'.

I don't know if there's something here or not. But it may be time to revisit this argument from the perspective of the Simulation Argument[61] and the physics of qualia & valence. Likewise, any serious treatment of the Simulation Argument absolutely *must* pay attention to qualia & valence.

---

v1.0: Initial release, 11-16-16
v1.01: Fixed various spelling errors & added a footnote in Sec. XII, 1-16-17

---

[61] This may also offer somewhat of a basis for a probability measure for Tegmark's set of Level IV multiverses.

Citations:

Aaronson, Scott. 2014a. "Why I Am Not An Integrated Information Theorist (or, The Unconscious Expander)." *Schtetl-Optimized.* April 21. http://www.scottaaronson.com/blog/?p=1799.
———. 2014b. "'Could a Quantum Computer Have Subjective Experience?'" *Shtetl-Optimized.* August 25. http://www.scottaaronson.com/blog/?p=1951.
———. 2016. "The Ghost in the Quantum Turing Machine." In *Computing the World*, edited by S. Barry Cooper and Andrew Hodges, 193–296. Cambridge University Press.
Albantakis, Larissa, Hintze Arend, Koch Christof, Adami Christoph, and Giulio Tononi. 2014. "Evolution of Integrated Causal Structures in Animats Exposed to Environments of Increasing Complexity." *PLoS Computational Biology* 10 (12): e1003966.
Atasoy, Selen, Isaac Donnelly, and Joel Pearson. 2016. "Human Brain Networks Function in Connectome-Specific Harmonic Waves." *Nature Communications* 7 (January): 10340.
Baars, Bernard J. 1988. "An Attempted Philosophy of Information." *PsycCRITIQUES* 33 (11). doi:10.1037/026215.
———. 2005. "Global Workspace Theory of Consciousness: Toward a Cognitive Neuroscience of Human Experience." In *Progress in Brain Research*, 45–53.
Balduzzi, David, and Giulio Tononi. 2008. "Integrated Information in Discrete Dynamical Systems: Motivation and Theoretical Framework." *PLoS Computational Biology* 4 (6): e1000091.
———. 2009. "Qualia: The Geometry of Integrated Information." *PLoS Computational Biology* 5 (8): e1000462.
Barrett, Adam B. 2014. "An Integration of Integrated Information Theory with Fundamental Physics." *Frontiers in Psychology* 5 (February): 63.
Barrett, Lisa Feldman. 2006. "Are Emotions Natural Kinds?" *Perspectives on Psychological Science: A Journal of the Association for Psychological Science* 1 (1): 28–58.
Berridge, Kent C., and Morten L. Kringelbach. 2013. "Neuroscience of Affect: Brain Mechanisms of Pleasure and Displeasure." *Current Opinion in Neurobiology* 23 (3): 294–303.
Berridge, Kent C., Terry E. Robinson, and J. Wayne Aldridge. 2009. "Dissecting Components of Reward: 'liking', 'wanting', and Learning." *Current Opinion in Pharmacology* 9 (1): 65–73.
Bischoff-Grethe, Amanda, Eliot Hazeltine, Lindsey Bergren, Richard B. Ivry, and Scott T. Grafton. 2009. "The Influence of Feedback Valence in Associative Learning." *NeuroImage* 44 (1): 243–51.
Bostrom, Nick. 2003. "Are We Living in a Computer Simulation?" *The Philosophical Quarterly* 53 (211): 243–55.
Brembs, Björn. 2011. "Towards a Scientific Concept of Free Will as a Biological Trait: Spontaneous Actions and Decision-Making in Invertebrates." *Proceedings. Biological Sciences / The Royal Society* 278 (1707): 930–39.
Buchheim, Christoph, and Michael Jünger. 2004. "An Integer Programming Approach to Fuzzy Symmetry Detection." In *Lecture Notes in Computer Science*, edited by Giuseppe Liotta, 2912:166–77. Lecture Notes in Computer Science. Springer Berlin Heidelberg.
Bullmore, Ed, and Olaf Sporns. 2009. "Complex Brain Networks: Graph Theoretical Analysis of Structural and Functional Systems." *Nature Reviews. Neuroscience* 10 (3): 186–98.
Buzsaki, Gyorgy. 2006. *Rhythms of the Brain.* Oxford University Press.
Carlsson, Gunnar. 2009. "Topology and Data." *Bulletin of the American Mathematical Society* 46 (2): 255–308.
Carroll, Sean. 2011. "The Eternally Existing, Self-Reproducing, Frequently Puzzling Inflationary Universe." *Cosmic Variance.* October 21. http://blogs.discovermagazine.com/cosmicvariance/2011/10/21/the-eternally-existing-self-reproducing-frequently-puzzling-inflationary-universe/.
———. 2016. "Consciousness and Downward Causation." *Preposterous Universe.* September 8. http://www.preposterousuniverse.com/blog/2016/09/08/consciousness-and-downward-causation/.
Casali, Adenauer G., Olivia Gosseries, Mario Rosanova, Mélanie Boly, Simone Sarasso, Karina R. Casali, Silvia Casarotto, et al. 2013. "A Theoretically Based Index of Consciousness Independent of Sensory Processing and Behavior." *Science Translational Medicine* 5 (198): 198ra105.
Cerullo, Michael. 2016. "Is Consciousness Just a State of Matter? A Critique of the Theory of Perceptronium." presented at the TSC 2016 Tucson: The Science of Consciousness (poster session), Tucson, Arizona, April 25. http://www.consciousness.arizona.edu/documents/TSC2016_BOOK_of_Abstracts_final.pdf.
Cerullo, Michael A. 2015. "The Problem with Phi: A Critique of Integrated Information Theory." *PLoS Computational Biology* 11 (9): e1004286.
Chalmers, David J. 1995. "The Puzzle of Conscious Experience." *Scientific American* 273 (6): 80–86.
———. 2008. "Strong and Weak Emergence." In *The Re-Emergence of Emergence*, 244–54.

Chon, Song Hui. 2008. "Quantifying the Consonance of Complex Tones with Missing Fundamentals." Edited by Julius O. Smith. MA, Stanford University. https://ccrma.stanford.edu/~shchon/pubs/shchon-thesis-final.pdf.

Clark, Andy. 2013. "Whatever next? Predictive Brains, Situated Agents, and the Future of Cognitive Science." *The Behavioral and Brain Sciences* 36 (3): 181–204.

Clore, Gerald L., Karen Gasper, and Ericka Garvin. 2001. "Affect as Information." In *Handbook of Affect and Social Cognition*, edited by J. P. Forgas, 121–44. Mahwah, NJ: Lawrence Erlbaum Associates.

Cohen, Michael A., Daniel C. Dennett, and Nancy Kanwisher. 2016. "What Is the Bandwidth of Perceptual Experience?" *Trends in Cognitive Sciences* 20 (5): 324–35.

Cooper, Jeffrey C., and Brian Knutson. 2008. "Valence and Salience Contribute to Nucleus Accumbens Activation." *NeuroImage* 39 (1): 538–47.

Cosmides, Leda. 2011. "The Architecture of Motivation." presented at the Edge Master Class 2011: The Science of Human Nature., Napa, California, July. https://www.edge.org/conversation/leda_cosmides-the-architecture-of-motivation-edgemaster-class-2011.

Cromwell, Howard C., and Kent C. Berridge. 1993. "Where Does Damage Lead to Enhanced Food Aversion: The Ventral Pallidum/substantia Innominata or Lateral Hypothalamus?" *Brain Research* 624 (1-2): 1–10.

Dewall, C. Nathan, Geoff Macdonald, Gregory D. Webster, Carrie L. Masten, Roy F. Baumeister, Caitlin Powell, David Combs, et al. 2010. "Acetaminophen Reduces Social Pain: Behavioral and Neural Evidence." *Psychological Science* 21 (7): 931–37.

D'iakonova, V. E. 2001. "The role of opioid peptides in the invertebrate behavior." *Zhurnal evoliutsionnoi biokhimii i fiziologii* 37 (4): 253–61.

Dirac, P. A. M. 1931. "Quantised Singularities in the Electromagnetic Field." *Proceedings of the Royal Society A: Mathematical, Physical and Engineering Sciences* 133 (821): 60–72.

Drenth, Joost P. H., and Stephen G. Waxman. 2007. "Mutations in Sodium-Channel Gene SCN9A Cause a Spectrum of Human Genetic Pain Disorders." *The Journal of Clinical Investigation* 117 (12): 3603–9.

Durso, Geoffrey R. O., Andrew Luttrell, and Baldwin M. Way. 2015. "Over-the-Counter Relief From Pains and Pleasures Alike: Acetaminophen Blunts Evaluation Sensitivity to Both Negative and Positive Stimuli." *Psychological Science* 26 (6): 750–58.

Eldar, Eran, Robb B. Rutledge, Raymond J. Dolan, and Yael Niv. 2016. "Mood as Representation of Momentum." *Trends in Cognitive Sciences* 20 (1): 15–24.

Farah, Martha J. 2014. "Brain Images, Babies, and Bathwater: Critiquing Critiques of Functional Neuroimaging." *The Hastings Center Report* Spec No (March): S19–30.

Ferrarelli, Fabio, Marcello Massimini, Simone Sarasso, Adenauer Casali, Brady A. Riedner, Giuditta Angelini, Giulio Tononi, and Robert A. Pearce. 2010. "Breakdown in Cortical Effective Connectivity during Midazolam-Induced Loss of Consciousness." *Proceedings of the National Academy of Sciences of the United States of America* 107 (6): 2681–86.

Feynman, Richard P. 1965. "The Feynman Lectures on Physics; Vol. I." *American Journal of Physics* 33 (9): 750.

Fisher, Matthew. 2015. "Quantum Cognition: The Possibility of Processing with Nuclear Spins in the Brain." *Arxiv.org*. https://arxiv.org/abs/1508.05929.

Flanagan, Brian J. 2007. "Are Perceptual Fields Quantum Fields?" *NeuroQuantology: An Interdisciplinary Journal of Neuroscience and Quantum Physics* 1 (3). doi:10.14704/nq.2003.1.3.20.

Frijda, Nico H. 1988. "The Laws of Emotion." *The American Psychologist* 43 (5): 349–58.

Friston, Karl. 2010. "The Free-Energy Principle: A Unified Brain Theory?" *Nature Reviews. Neuroscience* 11 (2): 127–38.

Gomez Emilsson, Andres. 2015a. "Manifolds of Consciousness: The Emerging Geometries of Iterated Local Binding." *Qualiacomputing.com*. March 13. https://qualiacomputing.com/2015/03/13/manifolds-of-consciousness-the-emerging-geometries-of-iterated-local-binding/.

———. 2015b. "State-Space of Drug Effects: Results." *Qualiacomputing.com*. June 9. https://qualiacomputing.com/2015/06/09/state-space-of-drug-effects-results/.

———. 2016. "Algorithmic Reduction of Psychedelic States." *Qualiacomputing.com*. June 20. https://qualiacomputing.com/2016/06/20/algorithmic-reduction-of-psychedelic-states/.

Haun, Andrew M., Oizumi Masafumi, Christopher K. Kovach, Kawasaki Hiroto, Oya Hiroyuki, Matthew A. Howard, Adolphs Ralph, and Tsuchiya Naotsugu. 2016. "Contents of Consciousness Investigated as Integrated Information in Direct Human Brain Recordings." doi:10.1101/039032.

Heckert, Justin. 2012. "The Hazards of Growing Up Painlessly." *New York Times*, November 18.

Jensen, Jimmy, Andrew J. Smith, Matthäus Willeit, Adrian P. Crawley, David J. Mikulis, Irina Vitcu, and Shitij Kapur. 2007. "Separate Brain Regions Code for Salience vs. Valence during Reward Prediction in Humans." *Human*

Brain Mapping 28 (4): 294–302.

Joffily, Mateus, and Giorgio Coricelli. 2013. "Emotional Valence and the Free-Energy Principle." *PLoS Computational Biology* 9 (6): e1003094.

Johnson, Michael. 2015a. "Effective Altruism, and Building a Better QALY." *Opentheory.net*. June 4. http://opentheory.net/2015/06/effective-altruism-and-building-a-better-qaly/.

———. 2015b. "How Understanding Valence Could Help Make Future AIs Safer." *Opentheory.net*. September 28. http://opentheory.net/2015/09/fai_and_valence/.

Jonas, Eric, and Konrad Kording. 2016. "Could a Neuroscientist Understand a Microprocessor?" doi:10.1101/055624.

Kashdan, Todd B., Biswas-Diener Robert, and Laura A. King. 2008. "Reconsidering Happiness: The Costs of Distinguishing between Hedonics and Eudaimonia." *The Journal of Positive Psychology* 3 (4): 219–33.

Koch, Christof. 2015. Can Consciousness be Non-Biological? Interview by Robert Lawrence Kuhn. https://www.youtube.com/watch?v=XG-hpuhbSyo.

Kringelbach, Morten L., and Kent C. Berridge. 2009. "Towards a Functional Neuroanatomy of Pleasure and Happiness." *Trends in Cognitive Sciences* 13 (11): 479–87.

Leibniz, Gottfried. 1710 (1989). *Discourse on Metaphysics and Other Essays*. Hackett Publishing.

Lin, Henry W., and Max Tegmark. 2016. "Why Does Deep and Cheap Learning Work so Well?" http://arxiv.org/abs/1608.08225.

Marković, Danica, Radmilo Janković, and Ines Veselinović. 2015. "Mutations in Sodium Channel Gene SCN9A and the Pain Perception Disorders." *Advances in Anesthesiology* 2015: 1–6.

Massimini, Marcello, Fabio Ferrarelli, Reto Huber, Steve K. Esser, Harpreet Singh, and Giulio Tononi. 2005. "Breakdown of Cortical Effective Connectivity during Sleep." *Science* 309 (5744): 2228–32.

McCabe, Gordon. 2005. "Universe Creation on a Computer." *Studies in History and Philosophy of Science. Part B. Studies in History and Philosophy of Modern Physics* 36 (4): 591–625.

Mcdermott, Josh, and Marc Hauser. 2005. "The Origins of Music: Innateness, Uniqueness, and Evolution." *Music Perception* 23 (1): 29–59.

Morsella, Ezequiel. 2005. "The Function of Phenomenal States: Supramodular Interaction Theory." *Psychological Review* 112 (4): 1000–1021.

Nishikawa, Takashi, and Adilson E. Motter. 2016. "Symmetric States Requiring System Asymmetry." *Physical Review Letters* 117 (11): 114101.

Noether, Emmy. 1918. "Invariante Variationsprobleme." *Nachrichten von Der Gesellschaft Der Wissenschaften Zu Göttingen, Mathematisch-Physikalische Klasse* 1918: 235–57.

Oizumi, Masafumi, Larissa Albantakis, and Giulio Tononi. 2014. "From the Phenomenology to the Mechanisms of Consciousness: Integrated Information Theory 3.0." *PLoS Computational Biology* 10 (5). Public Library of Science: e1003588.

Oizumi, Masafumi, Shun-Ichi Amari, Toru Yanagawa, Naotaka Fujii, and Naotsugu Tsuchiya. 2016. "Measuring Integrated Information from the Decoding Perspective." *PLoS Computational Biology* 12 (1): e1004654.

Osteen, Jeremiah D., Volker Herzig, John Gilchrist, Joshua J. Emrick, Chuchu Zhang, Xidao Wang, Joel Castro, et al. 2016. "Selective Spider Toxins Reveal a Role for the Nav1.1 Channel in Mechanical Pain." *Nature* 534 (7608): 494–99.

Panksepp, Jaak. 2010. "Affective Neuroscience of the Emotional BrainMind: Evolutionary Perspectives and Implications for Understanding Depression." *Dialogues in Clinical Neuroscience* 12 (4): 533–45.

Penrose, Roger. 1989. "Difficulties with Inflationary Cosmology." *Annals of the New York Academy of Sciences* 571 (1 Texas Symposi): 249–64.

Safron, Adam. 2016. "What Is Orgasm? A Model of Sexual Trance and Climax via Rhythmic Entrainment." *Socioaffective Neuroscience & Psychology* 6 (0). doi:10.3402/snp.v6.31763.

Schmidhuber, Jürgen. 2009. "Driven by Compression Progress: A Simple Principle Explains Essential Aspects of Subjective Beauty, Novelty, Surprise, Interestingness, Attention, Curiosity, Creativity, Art, Science, Music, Jokes." In *Lecture Notes in Computer Science*, 48–76.

Schultz, Wolfram. 2015. "Neuronal Reward and Decision Signals: From Theories to Data." *Physiological Reviews* 95 (3): 853–951.

Schwitzgebel, Eric. 2012a Interview by Richard Marshall. http://www.3ammagazine.com/3am/the-splintered-skeptic/.

———. 2012b. "Why Tononi Should Allow That Conscious Entities Can Have Conscious Parts." *The Splintered Mind*. June 6. http://schwitzsplinters.blogspot.com/2012/06/why-tononi-should-rethink-his-rejection.html.

Seth, Anil K. 2013. "Interoceptive Inference, Emotion, and the Embodied Self." *Trends in Cognitive Sciences* 17 (11): 565–73.

Shriver, Adam. 2016. "The Unpleasantness of Pain For Humans and Other Animals."

https://www.academia.edu/12621257/The_Unpleasantness_of_Pain_For_Humans_and_Other_Animals.

Smith, Kyle S., Amy J. Tindell, J. Wayne Aldridge, and Kent C. Berridge. 2009. "Ventral Pallidum Roles in Reward and Motivation." *Behavioural Brain Research* 196 (2): 155–67.

Smolensky, Paul. 2006. "Harmony in Linguistic Cognition." *Cognitive Science* 30 (5): 779–801.

Snowdon, Charles T., and David Teie. 2010. "Affective Responses in Tamarins Elicited by Species-Specific Music." *Biology Letters* 6 (1): 30–32.

Storr, Anthony. 1992. *Music and the Mind*.

Tegmark, Max. 2000. "Importance of Quantum Decoherence in Brain Processes." *Physical Review. E, Statistical Physics, Plasmas, Fluids, and Related Interdisciplinary Topics* 61 (4 Pt B): 4194–4206.

———. 2007. "The Mathematical Universe." *Foundations of Physics. An International Journal Devoted to the Conceptual Bases and Fundamental Theories of Modern Physics* 38 (2): 101–50.

———. 2014a. *Our Mathematical Universe: My Quest for the Ultimate Nature of Reality*. Penguin UK.

———. 2014b. "Friendly Artificial Intelligence: The Physics Challenge." *Arxiv.org*. https://arxiv.org/pdf/1409.0813v2.pdf.

———. 2015. "Consciousness as a State of Matter." *Chaos, Solitons & Fractals* 76: 238–70.

———. 2016. "Improved Measures of Integrated Information." Arxiv.org. http://arxiv.org/pdf/1601.02626.pdf.

Thorngren, Ryan Ragnar. 2016. "Entropy as a Measure of Symmetry." *Topological Quantum Field Theory*. April 5. https://math.berkeley.edu/wp/tqft/entropy-as-a-measure-of-symmetry/.

Tononi, Giulio. 2012. "Integrated Information Theory of Consciousness: An Updated Account." *Archives Italiennes de Biologie* 150 (2-3): 56–90.

———. 2014. "Why Scott Should Stare at a Blank Wall and Reconsider (or, the Conscious Grid)." http://integratedinformationtheory.org/download/conscious_grid.pdf.

———. 2016 Interview by Michael Johnson.

Tononi, Giulio, and Larissa Albantakis. 2014. "Consciousness - Here, There, Everywhere? The Prospects for Panpsychism." presented at the Association for the Scientific Study of Consciousness Satellite Conference (ASSC 18), Byron Bay, Australia, July. https://www.youtube.com/watch?v=hE-gGAyXpAs.

Tononi, Giulio, and Christof Koch. 2015. "Consciousness: Here, There and Everywhere?" *Philosophical Transactions of the Royal Society of London. Series B, Biological Sciences* 370 (1668). doi:10.1098/rstb.2014.0167.

Trainor, Laurel J., Christine D. Tsang, and Vivian H. W. Cheung. 2002. "Preference for Sensory Consonance in 2- and 4-Month-Old Infants." *Music Perception* 20 (2): 187–94.

Tsuchiya, Naotsugu, Shigeru Taguchi, and Hayato Saigo. 2016. "Using Category Theory to Assess the Relationship between Consciousness and Integrated Information Theory." *Neuroscience Research* 107 (June): 1–7.

Tsuchiya, Naotsugu, Melanie Wilke, Stefan Frässle, and Victor A. F. Lamme. 2015. "No-Report Paradigms: Extracting the True Neural Correlates of Consciousness." *Trends in Cognitive Sciences* 19 (12): 757–70.

Tymoczko, Dmitri. 2006. "The Geometry of Musical Chords." *Science* 313 (5783): 72–74.

Uttal, William R. 2011. *Mind and Brain: A Critical Appraisal of Cognitive Neuroscience*. MIT Press.

Van Orman Quine, Willard. 1964. *Word and Object*. MIT Press.

Van Swinderen, B., and R. Andretic. 2011. "Dopamine in Drosophila: Setting Arousal Thresholds in a Miniature Brain." *Proceedings of the Royal Society B: Biological Sciences* 278 (1707): 906–13.

Weyl, Hermann. 1952. *Symmetry*. Princeton University Press.

Wigner, Eugene. 1967. "Symmetries and Reflections, Scientific Essays." *American Journal of Physics* 35 (12): 1169.

Wigner, Eugene P. 1960. "The Unreasonable Effectiveness of Mathematics in the Natural Sciences. Richard Courant Lecture in Mathematical Sciences Delivered at New York University, May 11, 1959." *Communications on Pure and Applied Mathematics* 13 (1): 1–14.

Wilczek, Frank. 2015. *A Beautiful Question: Finding Nature's Deep Design*. Penguin.

Witek, Maria A. G., Eric F. Clarke, Mikkel Wallentin, Morten L. Kringelbach, and Peter Vuust. 2014. "Syncopation, Body-Movement and Pleasure in Groove Music." *PloS One* 9 (4): e94446.

Wittgenstein, Ludwig. 1922. *Tractatus Logico-Philosophicus*.

———. 1953. *Philosophical Investigations*.

Printed in Poland
by Amazon Fulfillment
Poland Sp. z o.o., Wrocław